MW00877412

Restoring Shared Prosperity:
A Policy Agenda from Leading Keynesian Economists

edited by

Thomas I. Palley and Gustav A. Horn

Published December 2013

ISBN-10: 1493749420
ISBN-13: 978-1493749423
LCCN: 2013923093

Table of Contents

List of Contributors

Dean Baker, Center for Economic and Policy Research, Washington, DC, USA.
Jared Bernstein, Center on Budget and Policy Priorities, Washington, DC, USA.
Josh Bivens, Economic Policy Institute, Washington, DC, USA.
Gerhard Bosch, University Duisburg-Essen and Director of the Institut Arbeit und Qualifikation, Duisberg-Essen, Germany.
Andreas Botsch, European Trade Union Institute (ETUI), Brussels, Belgium.
Michael Dauderstädt, Friedrich-Ebert Foundation (FES), Bonn, Germany.
Gerald Epstein, Department of Economics and Political Economy Research Institute (PERI), University of Massachusetts, Amherst, USA.
Heiner Flassbeck, University of Hamburg and Flassbeck-economics, Geneva, Switzerland.
Eckhard Hein, Berlin School of Economics and Law, Berlin, Germany.
Gustav A. Horn, Macroeconomics Policy Institute (IMK), Hans-Böckler Foundation, Dusseldorf, Germany.
Thomas I. Palley, AFL-CIO, Washington, DC, USA.
Robert Pollin, Department of Economics and Political Economy Research Institute (PERI), University of Massachusetts, Amherst, USA.
Jan Priewe, Department of Economics, HTW Berlin – University of Applied Sciences, Berlin, Germany.
John Schmitt, Center for Economic and Policy Research, Washington, DC, USA.
Heidi Shierholz, Economic Policy Institute, Washington, DC, USA.
Damon Silvers, AFL-CIO, Washington, DC, USA.
William E. Spriggs, AFL-CIO, Washington, DC, USA.
Jennifer S. Taub, Vermont Law School, South Royalton, Vermont, USA.
Silke Tober, Macroeconomics Policy Institute (IMK), Hans-Böckler Foundation, Dusseldorf, Germany.
Achim Truger, Berlin School of Economics and Law, Berlin, Germany.
Richard L. Trumka, AFL-CIO, Washington, DC, USA.

Foreword

This book is the product of two day-long conferences held in Washington, DC and Berlin on February 11 and March 11, 2013 respectively. The theme was "A trans-Atlantic agenda for shared prosperity". The Washington conference was held at the headquarters of the AFL-CIO, and the Berlin conference was held at the headquarters of the Friedrich Ebert Foundation.

The Washington conference was opened by Richard L. Trumka, President of the AFL-CIO. His opening remarks have been included as chapter 1 and they show clearly the importance of economic ideas for both economic policy and society's larger socio-political vision.

The two conferences were spurred by recognition of the troubling economic conditions in the US and Europe, both with regard to macroeconomic performance and with regard to income distribution and the outlook for shared prosperity. These troubling conditions have already created great suffering for many and, if unaddressed, they have the potential to unleash ugly political developments.

In the US, the economic recovery since the Great Recession has remained sub-par and beset by persistent fear that it might weaken again. Even if that is avoided, the most likely outcome is continued weak growth, accompanied by high unemployment and historically high levels of income inequality. In Europe, the recovery from the Great Recession has been even worse, with the euro zone beset by an unresolved euro crisis that has already contributed to a double-dip recession in the region.

This book offers an alternative agenda for shared prosperity to that on offer from mainstream economists. The thinking is rooted in the Keynesian analytic tradition, which we believe has been substantially vindicated by events. However, pure Keynesian macroeconomic analysis is supplemented by a focus on the institutions and policy interventions needed for an economy to generate a pattern of income distribution and demand consistent with productive full employment with contained income inequality. Such a perspective can be termed "structural Keynesianism".

We invite mainstream economists to engage in debate with the perspective and policies presented in this book. These are critical times and the public deserves an open debate that does not arbitrarily or ideologically lock out alternative perspectives and policy ideas.

We hope that the general public, politicians, and policymakers will find a credible policy program for shared prosperity, rooted in a clear narrative that cuts through the economic confusions that currently bedevil debate.

We thank the AFL-CIO, the Friedrich Ebert Foundation, and the Hans Böckler Foundation's Institute for Macroeconomic Policy for financial support for the conferences. We also thank Pia Bungarten (Director of the

Friedrich Ebert Foundation's Washington Office) and Knut Panknin (Program Officer with the Friedrich Ebert Foundation's Washington Office) for their help organizing both the Washington and Berlin conferences. Lastly, we thank Jamie Baker for setting the manuscript and organizing its publication.

Thomas I. Palley
Senior Economic Policy Adviser, AFL-CIO

Gustav A. Horn
Director, Macroeconomic Policy Institute

I
The War of Ideas

1. The War of Ideas and the Clash of Values

Richard L. Trumka is President of the AFL-CIO. These remarks were delivered at the opening of the "Trans-Atlantic Agenda for Shared Prosperity" conference held in Washington, DC at the AFL-CIO on February 11, 2013.

Good morning everyone. Welcome to the AFL-CIO.

I want to begin by thanking Pia Bungarten of the Friedrich Ebert Foundation (FES) and Gustav Horn of the Macroeconomics Institute of the Hans Böckler Foundation for partnering with the AFL-CIO in sponsoring today's conference. Today's conference is the first of two international meetings sponsored by the AFL-CIO, the FES, and the Hans Böckler Foundation. The second meeting will be in Berlin on March 11.

It is very fitting that today's conference is about a Trans-Atlantic agenda for shared prosperity. The Trans-Atlantic economy is the world's largest economic bloc, and Europe and the United States have a long history of productive economic engagement.

As you can see from the program, we have assembled an outstanding group of economists to speak on issues of critical import for full employment and shared prosperity. And at lunchtime we will hear from two extremely distinguished policymakers – Janet Yellen, Vice Chair of the Federal Reserve, and Matthias Machnig, Minister of Economy for the German Federal State of Thuringia. The AFL-CIO is deeply honored to have the privilege of hosting such a distinguished gathering of economic thinkers.

Five years ago the US economy descended into a financial crisis that went on to shake the foundations of the entire global economy. At its peak in 2008 there were fears the world was on the verge of a second Great Depression.

Fortunately, key policymakers around the world had absorbed the lessons of the Great Depression, and understood the role that poor policy choices played in that catastrophe. During 2008 and 2009, guided by the insights of John Maynard Keynes, policymakers took courageous fiscal and monetary policy actions that stopped us from spiraling into depression.

Then three years ago policymakers changed course, first in Europe, then in the United States. Government after government, encouraged by the IMF and the OECD, embraced the idea that austerity—cutting government spending and public employment—was the right medicine for economies suffering from slow growth, mass unemployment, and recession driven deficits. In economy after economy, and most recently the US economy, austerity policies have led to relapses into negative growth. Today the IMF and the OECD are rethinking this approach. Today's meeting is about assessing this recent history and looking for alternatives to policies that bleed the patient.

Here in the United States, there is no question that we have made progress stabilizing the situation and reversing some of the damage. Most importantly, we have had almost four years of employment growth. We have now surpassed the level of private sector employment prior to President Obama taking office.

But it has not been easy. We have had to battle those who wanted to block the fiscal stimulus that was so critical for stopping the economic slide. And we are still battling those same people who now want to impose fiscal austerity that risks sabotaging the economy and triggering a new recession, as those same policies have in Europe.

A similar struggle has occurred over monetary policy, where we have had to battle those who first argued against the Federal Reserve lowering interest rates; then argued against the Federal Reserve engaging in quantitative easing; and now want the Federal Reserve to prematurely end its policies aimed at stimulating economic activity.

These policy battles illustrate the critical significance of economics and of economic policy for shared prosperity and full employment.

But there is a far bigger lesson, which is that in economic policy, ideas matter. We are engaged in a war of ideas as well as a clash of values and interests.

But the war of ideas is much bigger than the debate about stimulus. It extends to the larger terrain of how we explain the crisis and how we need to change our economy.

Some argue the crisis was simply due to a financial shock that caused an unusually deep recession. From this point of view, all that is needed is financial sector reform to deal with the cause of the shock plus a large dose of stimulus to escape the recession. Nothing else needs to change because the rest of the economic model is supposedly fine. This sort of *status quo* reformer argues that our economic policy goal should be to go back to the way it was before the financial crisis and the Great Recession.

That is not the view of the American labor movement. Things were badly wrong with the American economy long before the crisis. The financial crisis was just the crowning event that brought those failings into full focus.

For over thirty years we experienced wage stagnation and we masked the gap between rising output and stagnant wages with a sea of credit that maintained spending and kept employment up. The evidence was crystal clear before 2008—the results of these policy-driven trends were global imbalances, long term wage stagnation, rising inequality and insecurity, and repeated financially driven economic crises.

However, Wall Street and corporate money flooded politics and think-tanks to buy influence and authority that sold fake "credit bubble" prosperity as real prosperity, and sold falling wages and rising profits as the inevitable reward to technological change and global competition rather than old fashioned greed and rigging the shape of economy. And tragically, their voices won out and the financial crisis came.

That financial crisis made it possible to tell the real story. And the story of how wage stagnation and increased income inequality cracked our economic foundation is now heard throughout the land, and is widely accepted both by scholars and the public.

Yet here in Washington, Wall Street and the beneficiaries of income inequality are trying to do everything they can to block this growing understanding. Their goal is to double-down on policies like trickle-down economics that have harmed us so badly.

Because this is the reality of Washington, today's event—a serious cross border examination of the challenge of economic revival, could not be more important. We must explore and explain the policies that can restore full employment with shared prosperity. Winning the war of ideas requires both explaining what went wrong and how to remedy the situation.

We cannot change the past, but if we win the war of ideas we can change the course of the future.

That is the agenda today. The speakers you will hear from will explain:

- The role of macroeconomic policy in sustaining the recovery and investing in a future of shared prosperity;
- How to make finance serve the real economy instead of having the real economy serve finance;
- How to design labor markets that raise wages and restore the link between wages and productivity growth;
- And how to fashion the relation between market and government so that people have the security and wherewithal to invest in themselves, their families, and their communities.

And now, let me turn the floor over to this morning's first panel.

Thank you.

2. The War of Ideas: A Comparison of the US and Europe

Thomas I. Palley, Senior Economic Policy Adviser, AFL-CIO, mail@thomaspalley.com.

Ideas matter

The financial crisis of 2008, the Great Recession it triggered, and the great stagnation that followed, have spawned a "war of ideas". On both sides of the Atlantic, progressives and trade unionists are engaged in a struggle, the outcome of which will greatly influence the future.

The war of ideas is present in the debate over whether fiscal and monetary stimulus is the right policy response to the crisis, or whether the right response is fiscal austerity and rejection of quantitative easing by central banks. The war of ideas is also reflected in the explanation we give for the crisis.

In the US there are three competing explanations (Palley, 2012, chapter 3). The first is the hardcore neoliberal explanation that can be labeled the government failure hypothesis. According to it, the crisis is due to the implosion of a house price bubble caused by the Federal Reserve and government housing policy. The Federal Reserve supposedly pushed interest rates too low and held them there too long in the period 2001 – 2007, while politically motivated government intervention in the home mortgage market encouraged unwise and unsupportable levels of home ownership.

The second explanation is the softcore neoliberal explanation which can be labeled the market failure hypothesis. According to it, the crisis is the result of a financial implosion caused by the combination of excessive financial deregulation, lax financial regulation that permitted dangerous speculation, and so-called "black swan" effects resulting from excessive financial complexity.

The third explanation is the structural Keynesian "destruction of shared prosperity hypothesis" whereby the crisis is the logical outcome of thirty years of neoliberal policy. Those policies caused wage stagnation and widened income inequality, the adverse effects of which were papered over by a generation long credit bubble that eventually burst.

In Europe, there are also three explanations for the euro zone's crisis. The first is it is a public debt crisis caused by government fiscal profligacy (Lachman, 2010). The second is it is a balance of payments crisis caused by Germany's pursuit of export-led growth based on domestic wage suppression which has undermined both European aggregate demand and the competitiveness and sustainability of Southern Europe's economies (Bibow, 2013). The third is it is the result of Europe's adoption of a neoliberal policy regime that undermined aggregate demand by creating wage stagnation. Europe's policymakers also implemented a flawed design for the euro that created a form of analogue gold standard, thereby exposing countries to the types of financial fragility that afflicted the gold standard a century earlier (Palley, 2013).

The war of ideas is relevant to both Europe and the US because how we explain the crisis will determine how we respond to it. It is already affecting the character of the monetary and fiscal policy response, and it will also affect the content and direction of future policy.

If you accept the hardcore neoliberal position, the recommended policy response is fiscal austerity now and "doubling-down" on the neoliberal policies of the past thirty years. Those policies include more deregulation of financial and product markets; deepening the laissez-faire version of globalization; shrinking government and social welfare protections; more flexibilizing of labor markets by dismantling unions, worker protections, and the minimum wage; and strict inflation targeting. From a hardcore neoliberal standpoint, the crisis proves prior neoliberal reforms were not pure enough, which prevented the market from functioning properly.

If you accept the softcore neoliberal position the recommendation is to modernize financial regulation to avoid a repeat of the financial crisis of 2008. In addition, because the crisis caused a deep recession, large-scale monetary and fiscal stimulus is needed to jumpstart the economy again. However, once recovery is on track, fiscal austerity and downsizing of the welfare state will be needed to offset fiscal stimulus expended. Other than that, little else needs change as the basic neoliberal economic model is sound.

Lastly, if you accept the structural Keynesian destruction of shared prosperity hypothesis the policy recommendation is stimulus now plus structural reform that reverses the neoliberal attack on workers and social democratic government. That means establishing rules for globalization that prevent an international race to the bottom; restoring full employment as a key policy objective of macroeconomic policy; rebuilding labor market institutions like unions and the minimum wage that ensure wage are tied to productivity growth; and restoring social democratic government that provides public goods, education, health care, and a basic level of retirement income security.

These different recommended policy responses to the crisis show the importance of ideas. How the crisis is explained and interpreted will affect the choices society makes in response. That makes the war of ideas critical.

The war of ideas in the US and Europe: a comparison

Because neoliberalism is a global ideology, the war of ideas is being fought on a global scale. However, the terrain and challenges differs across countries because history, politics, and culture differ across countries. It is therefore interesting to compare the challenge in Europe, exemplified by Germany, with that in the United States.

The state of the policy debate

In Germany, mainstream political opinion (Christian Democrats versus Social Democrats) appears less divided. That is reflected in the relatively small differences that characterized the recent (2013) election contest between the incumbent Christian Democrat Chancellor, Angela Merkel, and the Social Democratic challenger, former Finance Minister Peer Steinbrück. In Germany, the microeconomic social contract about the strong merits of the welfare state remains largely intact. However, the macroeconomic social contract about the role and significance of counter-cyclical Keynesian policy has been largely discarded by both sides of the political aisle.

In the US, political opinion is much more sharply divided, as reflected in the vitriolic challenge waged by Republicans against the Obama administration. The microeconomic social contract about the welfare state is under profound attack, with the Republicans seeking to annihilate it completely. A small but powerful group of Democrats is also willing to go along with shrinking its scope and depth. However, the macroeconomic social contract about Keynesian counter-cyclical policy remains intact. Democrats are strong supporters but, surprisingly, so too are Republicans. It is easy to be fooled by Republican rhetoric against counter-cyclical policy and their obstruction of the Obama administration's requests for fiscal stimulus. However, that reflects tactical politics aimed at sabotaging the Obama administration. If Republicans were in power they would use plutocratic counter-cyclical policy, as they did in the recession of 2001 under President George W. Bush. Their current opposition to fiscal stimulus derives from a combination of opposition to egalitarian counter-cyclical policy plus a desire for President Obama to fail.

In a sense, Europe and the US are symmetric opposites. Debate is more contested in the US and the microeconomic welfare state social contract is under attack. Debate is less contested in Germany and it is the macroeconomic counter-cyclical social contract that is under attack.

The state of understanding

In the US, neoliberal opposition is far stronger and success requires much deeper change regarding society's views about the economy. Neoliberal "free market" ideology has taken much deeper root in the public's political imagination, making it harder to reverse. Contrastingly, in Europe the dominant social and intellectual ethos remains social democratic. What is needed is that Social Democrats rediscover their social democratic heart and belief in the merits of both the microeconomic and macroeconomic social contract.

In many regards, the challenge posed by the war of ideas is greater in the US than in Europe. That is because neoliberalism has deeper roots in American culture and the American public's imagination. But even though the overall challenge is greater, the direction of movement is also more favorable. In the US political engagement has at least begun, as evidenced by the more vitriolic political discourse. In Germany and Europe it has not, as measured by the very modest differences of political style and program. Across the continent, Social Democrats have shied away from offering a substantively different explanation of the economic crisis with a correspondingly different policy program.

There is a lot of complaint about the contested and divided nature of US political discourse. Those complaints are misplaced. At this historical moment, contest and division is a good thing, not a bad thing. It is the hallmark of the beginning of change. If anything, the problem is Democrats have not differentiated themselves enough from Republicans and have not yet offered policies that match the scale of the problem.

Current dangers

It is also the case that Europe is in a more dangerous position. In the US economic growth is sub-par but it is positive, employment has increased substantially since the end of the recession in 2009, and there is nothing equivalent to the euro zone crisis. In contrast, Europe is trapped in stagnation and has experienced double-dip recession. The periphery countries of Greece, Ireland, and Portugal are in depression. So too is Spain, which is Europe's fourth largest economy. Italy is in teetering on renewed recession and financial markets have grave doubts about the state of Italy's public finances. Economic conditions and public finances are weakening in France, and the UK has also experienced a double-dip recession and appears stuck with near zero growth. Even Germany is in a dangerous situation as it is significantly oriented to export-led growth, which exposes it to European stagnation. It is also exposed to slowing growth in China.

These conditions are objectively bad enough. But things could get far worse if the euro disintegrates under country economic and political pressures. In that event, the economic and political fallout could be very ugly. That makes it urgent that European Social Democrats take up engagement with war of ideas.

Though the neoliberal impulse is weaker and the social democratic impulse stronger, Europe faces special political challenges because individual countries do not have the same level of control over their economic futures as the United States. That is because of the euro and monetary union. The euro needs reform but that is a European level task. In particular, the European Central Bank must take on the role of government banker for euro member countries so that it acts like the Federal Reserve already does on behalf of the US government. The role of government banker is to help the government manage its debts and finance budget deficits at reasonable interest rates.[1]

Second, given the lack of a single national government for the continent, Europe needs to introduce shared rules to ensure fiscal and wage coordination across countries. In slumps, countries must engage in coordinated fiscal stimulus. And in normal times wages must grow at roughly the same pace to discourage countries from engaging in a deflationary race to the bottom aimed at gaining competitiveness.

Third, Germany must be weaned from its export-led growth model based on wage suppression. As Europe's largest economy, Germany must shift to a domestic demand-led growth model based on rising wages so that it can play its proper role of locomotive for larger European economy.

These are massive political challenges. They require agreement among countries. They also require Germany's agreement as only Germany can change its own policies. That means the future of shared prosperity in Europe depends significantly on Germany's willingness to change and adopt a new European economic model. Unfortunately, even though German voters have a strong social democratic inclination, German political elites may be the most neoliberal in Europe.

Europe's global significance in the war of ideas

Europe's political history and culture makes it intrinsically less neoliberal. At the same time, it faces far greater political and institutional obstacles because of its fragmented governance structure.

---

[1] That will require introducing some form of euro bond, the revenues from which and the attached obligations are shared among all governments. Only such an arrangement can ensure that the European Central Bank treats countries equally and is not drawn into unfairly assisting individual countries at the expense of others.

Unfortunately, Europe's economic under-performance has major global consequences in the war of ideas. That is because Europe is widely viewed as the standard bearer of social democracy and Keynesianism. Thus, in public debate the European economic model is often posited as the social democratic alternative to the neoliberal US economic model. Consequently, when Europe fails, neoliberals use that failure to argue that social democratic Keynesianism does not work.

The great tragedy is that Europe's failure is self-inflicted. It is failing because Europe's policymakers have been even more captured by neoliberal macroeconomic policies than the United States. The European Central Bank (ECB) and European finance ministries are dominated by economic policymakers trained in Chicago school neoliberal economics. In contrast, the pragmatism of US politicians has supported budget deficits and Keynesianism. In the past that has held for both Republican and Democratic administrations though, recently, Republicans have become fiscal policy obstructionists as part of their strategy for wounding President Obama.

In economics, macroeconomic policy trumps microeconomic policy. Consequently, Europe's adoption of hardcore neoliberal macroeconomic policy has trumped its more social democratic microeconomic policy. As a result, the European economy has under-performed the US economy, giving rise to perceived failure of the social democratic model when it has not been given a chance to succeed.

The true measure of the social democratic model is the period 1950 – 1980 when Europe pursued a combination of Keynesian macroeconomic policies and social democratic microeconomic policies. That era was a golden age for Europe and the European model was shown to deliver. The past thirty years saw European policymakers abandon Keynesian inclinations. That undercut Europe's economic performance and under-mined the appeal of the European model, making it harder to challenge the neoliberal model.

Conclusion: a better future is possible

Neoliberalism is a global ideology that has infected the US, Europe, and Germany. From a structural Keynesian standpoint, neoliberal economic policy design is the ultimate cause of the global slump. The global challenge is to bend the arc of history away from neoliberalism and back toward social democratic Keynesianism that has proved capable of delivering shared prosperity and full employment. Meeting this challenge requires winning the war of ideas.

Just over 30 years ago wages started to stagnate and income inequality started to explode in both the US and Europe. A big reason was working families lost the war of ideas. The economic crisis provides an historic opportunity to reverse that defeat and thereby enable the restoration of shared prosperity and full employment. It can be done.

References

Bibow, J. (2012), "The euro debt crisis and Germany's euro trilemma," Working paper No. 721, Levy Economics Institute of Bard College, Annandale-on-Hudson, New York.

Lachman, D. (2010), "Euro will unravel, and soon: collapse could imperil US economy," American Enterprise Institute for Public Policy Research, Washington, DC, No. 2, September.

Palley, T.I. (2012), *From Financial Crisis to Stagnation: The Destruction of Shared Prosperity and the Role of Economics*, Cambridge: Cambridge University Press.

Palley, T.I. (2013), "Europe's crisis without end: the consequences of neoliberalism," *Contributions to Political Economy*, 32, 29-50.

3. Hypocritical Versus Hippocratic Economics

Andreas Botsch, *European Trade Union Institute (ETUI), Brussels, abotsch@etui.org.*

> "The ideas of economists and political philosophers, both when they are right and when they are wrong, are more powerful than is commonly understood. Indeed, the world is ruled by little else. Practical men, who believe themselves to be quite exempt from any intellectual influences, are usually the slaves of some defunct economist." (JM Keynes 1936, 383)

Introduction

Cambridge Dictionaries Online defines hypocrisy, as a 'situation in which someone pretends to believe something that they do not really believe, or that is the opposite of what they do or say'[1] . According to dictionary.com, it is the pretense of having virtues, beliefs, principles, that one does not actually possess. Wikipedia adds that hypocrisy involves the deception of others and is thus a kind of lie. European economic policy has plenty of it. In fact, except for a very short period of Keynesian policy response to what threatened to become a Great Depression, European economics (and the political leadership in charge of implementing them) has been little else than hypocritical. Neoliberal hypocritical economics pretends to do good for all while imposing harm on working people and their families. The theoretical justification is that 'it's got to get worse before it gets better'. However, the reality is that it has gotten significantly better for few and a lot worse for the many.

This implies an essential lesson for progressives and organized labor. The war of ideas requires them to equip themselves with knowledge of the war's historical roots and the ideological sources of present discourse and policy. This constitutes a necessary condition to even take up the challenge, let alone to win the war. This chapter identifies seven deadly hypocrisies that block an agenda for shared prosperity.

---

[1] http://dictionary.cambridge.org/dictionary/british/hypocrisy

Seven deadly hypocrisies

It all started when monetarist and new classical ideas acquired intellectual and political dominance in the late 1970's by depicting the previous 30-40 years of shared prosperity, inspired by the Keynesian consensus, as old-fashioned, ideologically flawed, and based on empirically inconsistent ideas. Contrary to Keynesian claims, they argued there was no trade-off between unemployment and inflation, and the high unemployment that accompanied the stagflation crisis of the 1970's could not be remedied by deficit spending. That would actually make it worse, so they said.

This change in thinking drove a new policy war against inflation, and once the anti-inflationists were politically in control, market liberalism became the new mainstream conventional wisdom. On both sides of the North Atlantic, neoliberals proclaimed the victory of market efficiency and declared that Keynesian-social thinking was dead.

The systemic financial crisis of 2008 and the ensuing Great Recession imploded the central ideas of market neoliberalism. But rather than fading away, the dead ideas of neoliberalism still walk among us as a form of zombie economics (Quiggin 2010).

#1: debt and austerity hypocrisies.

One of the most popular, but also most dangerous ideas of zombie economics has been fiscal austerity that disregards business cycle conditions (Blyth 2013). In modern capitalist history, austerity has been a recurring recipe in the slump. However, in practice it has never achieved its goal of debt reduction. Austerians tend to largely ignore the fallacy of composition effects of their policy prescriptions, whereby attempts to save by government simply lower aggregate demand and income, thereby lowering private saving. Furthermore, austerity has always made the poor pay for the mistakes of the rich. This is precisely what we have witnessed in the five years since the financial crisis, and the learning curve has been stunningly flat. The Keynesian re-birth in the immediate aftermath of the crisis was so short-lived that it lasted for only 18 months.

Why do these dead ideas, that support policies that have clearly failed, remain alive and kicking? Since the spring of 2010, the slogan has been "you cannot cure debt with more debt so start cutting and stop spending", and it remains the specter haunting the populations of the Western hemisphere. In German language, "debt" and "guilt" are homonyms. This is important because Germany has successfully imposed its agenda on the whole of Europe (even though it failed to impose fiscal debt brakes via the G20) and German policy is critical for crisis resolution in Europe. When spending is regarded as a sin, no politician wants to be identified as a profligate spender who allegedly lives at the expense of future generations. Telling wondrous stories, as the Germans do to the rest of the world, about the importance of everyone being thrifty ignores the paradox of thrift. When everyone tries to save more money during times of recession, aggregate demand and output will fall. The proof is seven consecutive quarters of recession in the euro area as a whole.

#2: the hypocrisy of confusing private and public debt sustainability.

When private households have accumulated debt that they cannot sustain, they need to reduce spending and borrowing to levels that make interest payments sustainable. That logic is falsely transferred to public debt. Politicians, such as German Chancellor Angela Merkel, proclaim public debt sustainability as equivalent to that of private households, with Merkel using the thrifty and virtuous Swabian housewife as an example for state budgets ("the Swabian housewife knows perfectly well that she cannot spend more than what she has saved before"). The morality play of micro-economics is used to make people believe that the venom is the cure. At the end of the treatment, the patient, in this case a united democratic Europe, might well decease. Too much venom, and both democracy and the Union may be laid to rest.

#3: public debt and growth hypocrisies.

Ash, Herndon and Pollin (2013) provide empirical evidence rejecting the research claims of Carmen Reinhart and Kenneth Rogoff concerning the relationship between public debt and GDP growth. They show that the Reinhart – Rogoff results were based on coding errors, selective exclusion of available data, and unconventional weighting of summary statistics. This led to serious errors that inaccurately represented the relationship between public debt and GDP growth among 20 advanced economies in the post-war period, particularly the claim that economies whose public debt to GDP ratios exceed 90 percent fall off a growth cliff.

Tragically, the now discredited Reinhart – Rogoff research had an immediate influence on top policymakers, including Manuel Barroso and Olli Rehn, President and Vice-President of the European Commission; German Chancellor Angela Merkel and her Finance Minister Wolfgang Schäuble; the Labor and Tory governments in the UK; and of course large parts of the political elite in Washington DC. Reinhart and Rogoff's purported 90 percent debt threshold provided austerians with an intellectual bazooka against anybody suggesting that the great balance sheet recession (Koo 2012) needed a more sustained fiscal stimulus to avoid a low growth stagnation outcome.

This history shows the dangerous consequences of economic thinking that is based on fictitious models rather than real world empirical facts.

#4: the profligate government hypocrisy and the abrogation of simple algebra.

According to the European Commission (EC 2011), private debt in Europe increased by more than 50 percent between 1999 and 2007 while government debt to GDP ratios fell across the EU. In contrast to widespread belief we have not seen government profligacy at all in the aftermath of the financial meltdown. What the North Atlantic world experienced was government taking over private debt by rescuing troubled banks and the capital assets of the wealthy. This enabled a great rechristening whereby the private debt crisis, caused by an allegedly efficient since deregulated financial sector gone mad, was now relabeled as a "sovereign debt crisis" caused by profligate governments in Southern Europe. This constitutes one of the "greatest bait and switch in modern history" (Blyth 2013, 73).

In fact, Greece was the sole European economy with profligate government spending, and it was assisted in its fiscal irresponsibility by Goldman Sachs which helped Greece's conservative government disguise its over-stretching of European fiscal rules. However, instead of being seen as a sample of one, Greece has been used to push the view that the European crisis is due to all peripheral country governments living beyond their means. That has provided a pretext to prescribe spending and wage cuts throughout Europe. However, slashing government spending in the midst of a downturn has only weakened aggregate demand, leading to further reduced output and employment.

The Greek crisis came as a welcome surprise guest to the table of Europe's neoliberal finance ministers. Instead of having to focus on repairing the damages inflicted by the financial sector and reducing the overhang of private debt to ease the painful deleveraging process of private households and enterprises, EU and G20 finance ministers were able to shift into reverse gear and reverse the fiscal stimulus. After rescuing the banks, public not private debt became the problem number one for them. Austerity was therefore unnecessarily self-imposed across the continent.

The conditions of the single currency acted as an additional burden – comparable to the gold standard that compelled EMU member states to adjust in the most painful of ways. Given the inability to effect nominal devaluations to adjust real effective exchange rates, countries were compelled to pursue internal devaluation via price and nominal wage deflation.

Application of basic algebra could have told the neoliberal hypocrites what the outcome would be. The simple truth is that the debt to GDP ratio has a denominator that cannot be ignored.

However, once again highly influential academic research was invoked to defend the austerian narrative. The "tales of fiscal adjustment" by Alesina and Ardagna (2010) found their way into high level meetings of EU finance ministers, where Alesina was invited to report on his findings. Alesina's idea of 'expansionary fiscal contraction' quickly made its way into speeches and official documents on economic policy of all European institutions, and served to defend expenditure cuts. The claim was cuts would improve business and consumer confidence, thereby strengthening the economy. And ever since, the confidence fairy has become the cornerstone of European economic policy.

#5: the rescue hypocrisy.

All the rescue packages for the 'program countries' (Greece, Ireland, Portugal, and Cyprus) bear harsh conditionality designed to implement internal devaluation. The new European Stability Mechanism, together with already disbursed and firmly committed programs for European economies in balance of payments crises, amount to more than one trillion euros.

These measures, along with Outright Monetary Transactions of the ECB, have temporarily stabilized European financial markets. However, they do not address the fundamental problem which is the lack a genuine central bank that is willing to act as government banker for the euro area and re-establish fiscal dominance (Palley 2011), and the lack of a European Treasury that can issue European sovereign debt and deal with European macro-economic imbalances.

Politically, the fundamental problem is not even discussed. Instead, people in the surplus Northern European economies are being told that they have to pay for 'lazy Southerners' in the periphery, whereas they are in fact rescuing capital assets of the wealthy across Europe and the banks. Moreover, some politicians have succumbed to the temptation of playing a divisive nationalist card, whereas solidarity is required to overcome the crisis.

#6: the competitiveness hypocrisy.

Europeans are being told to tighten their belts to become more competitive. One country after the other is receiving policy recommendations to cut wages and lower social standards against the others. Yet, this advice confronts the fallacy of composition. One country's gain in competitiveness is another's loss. Gaining competitiveness by pricing the unemployed back into the labor market is also equivalent to turning the victims into offenders.

Austerians, with their quasi-religious beliefs in Ricardian equivalence and the power of the confidence fairy to spur investment and growth, miss the essential point that we cannot all be austere at once. Private and public consumption are an essential part of aggregate demand. Unfortunately, across-the-board austerity is precisely what has been attempted in Europe, with huge social costs and a steep fall in European citizens' confidence in the European political elites.

#7: the financial market regulation hypocrisy.

Five years after the collapse of Lehman Brothers, thousands of pages of legislation intended to reform the financial sector have passed the votes in the European Parliament and the US Congress. However, most of the reforms undertaken so far have fallen short of tackling the core problems of the financial system – inspiring the illusion of market stability through more regulation which is not equal to better regulation.

To date, too-big, too-interconnected and too-complex-to-resolve banks are still alive. Fear of systemic risk has successfully jeopardized the aims of reconnecting risk and liability and of making creditors pay. Assets in European banks' balance sheets amount to more than 350% GDP, and as a result megabanks recovery and resolution is likely to require considerable public resources. Making finance serve society and the real economy necessitates a financial sector that is smaller in size, slower in speed, simpler in structure, separated functionally, less short-term oriented and, not least, democratized (Botsch 2011).

Conclusion

How would a fundamental change of policy look like? Many objections have been made to the neoliberal hypocrisies above. Yet economic policy would have to adopt a different approach by tackling neoliberal hypocrisies at their roots. Hippocrates is said to have authored the following rule for fellow physicians of his time: "The physician must be able to tell the antecedents, know the present, and foretell the future — must mediate these things, and have two special objects in view with regard to disease, namely, to do good or to do no harm" (Hippocrates 1849). Replace 'physician' by 'economist' and you have the basic principle of Hippocratic economics: first, do no harm.

It is of fundamental importance for a progressive agenda for shared prosperity that financialisation is abandoned and the curve of a falling wage share inverted. Full employment and decent jobs must move to the fore of economic policy. A stable system of finance serving society and the real economy, and a new global monetary system of stable currency exchange must be established (Payandeh 2011 and Priewe 2013 in this volume). Last, but not least, the abundance of excess liquidity on global markets must be channeled into sustainable, long-term investment, serving society as a whole.

The war of ideas must continue until prevailing hypocritical economics is replaced by Hippocratic economics.

References

Alberto Alesina and Silvia Ardagna (2010) Large Changes in Fiscal Policy: Taxes Versus Spending, Tax Policy and the Economy, Volume 24 (2010), The University of Chicago Press

Andreas Botsch (2011) Enhancing governance of financial markets through regulation: a ten point agenda; in Sigurt Vitols and Norbert Kluge, The Sustainable Company: a new approach to corporate governance, Brussels: ETUI, 227-244

Mark Blyth (2013), *Austerity: the history of a dangerous idea*, Oxford University Press

EC (European Commission) (2011), European economic forecast - autumn 2011, European Economy 6(2011), Brussels

Thomas Herndon, Michael Ash and Robert Pollin (2013), Does High Public Debt Consistently Stifle Economic Growth? A Critique of Reinhart and Rogoff, PERI Working Paper Series 322, University of Massachusetts Amherst, April 2013

Hippocrates (1849), Of the epidemics, Sect. II Second Constitution, translated by Francis Adams [1849], http://ebooks.adelaide.edu.au/h/hippocrates/epidemics/index.html

John Maynard Keynes (1936), *The General Theory of Employment, Interest and Money*, Cambridge University Press Macmillan, 1973

Richard Koo (2012), Balance Sheet Recession as the Other-Half of Macroeconomics, http://www.boeckler.de/pdf/v_2012_10_25_koo.pdf

Thomas Palley (2011), Euro lacks a government banker, not lender of last resort, Financial Times 9 December 2011, http://blogs.ft.com/economistsforum/2011/12/the-euro-lacks-a-government-banker-not-a-lender-of-last-resort/

Mehrdad Payandeh (2011) Outline of a new world currency system, Berlin and Brussels (mimeo)

John Quiggin (2010), *Zombie Economics: how dead ideas still walk among us*, New Jersey: Princeton University Press

Carmen Reinhart and Kenneth Rogoff (2010), Growth in Time of Debt, NBER Working Paper 15639, January 2010, http://www.nber.org/papers/w15639

4. The Great Failure: How Economics Must Change

Gustav Horn, Director, Macroeconomics Policy Institute (IMK), Hans-Böckler Foundation, Dusseldorf, Germany, gustav-horn@boeckler.de.

The Queen's question

"Why did no one see the crisis coming?" the Queen asked at a November 2008 gathering of prominent economists at the London School of Economics. Financial markets had already crashed at that point and the impact was starting to spread to the real economy on a global scale. In particular, banks developed a deep mistrust toward other banks and either refused to give money to them or would only lend at very high interest rates. Consequently, the whole credit process stopped. In particular, finance for investment and trade dried up, putting the global economy on course for the deepest recession since World War II (IMK, 2013).

Why did no mainstream economist see this coming? The basic answer is because mainstream economics assumes that free markets are essentially stable so that economic crisis is not part of standard theories or empirics. Mainstream economists therefore lacked the intellectual tools to understand the nature of what was happening in 2007 and 2008, as well as in the consecutive crisis of the Euro area.

David Collander (Collander et al., 2009) has called this a complete moral failure of economics. Economists knew how to deal with minor economic fluctuations, but failed to live up to the occasion when events became really serious. That is the core reason why economics has to change. Future economists should know that crisis can happen; they should know when danger is imminent; and they should know how to deal with it. This essay outlines some elements for that future economics.

The role of uncertainty

The basic failure of mainstream economics was the almost complete neglect of fundamental uncertainty (Skidelsky, 2010). Conventional models consider risk, which differs from uncertainty in that the probability distribution of risks is always known to agents. In situations of risk people know that events may not be certain, but they also know the nature of this uncertainty and can therefore take account of it when making decisions. In situations of fundamental uncertainty probability distributions simply do not exist. Unfortunately, economists applied the "risk" characterization of uncertainty to agents in financial markets. Agents were therefore assumed to understand the basic nature of risks so that they could reasonably limit their exposure to risk.

However, the 2008 financial market crisis revealed something different. Agents knew nothing about the nature of events after the Lehman crash. The result was they panicked and started to sell everything that seemed uncertain, pushing financial markets into an immediate deep plunge. At the same time, and for the very same reason, banks started to limit their willingness to provide credit, thereby providing a channel for the crisis in financial markets to spill over in to the real economy (De Grauwe and Ji, 2012).

This kind of contraction had not happened since the Great Depression. Keynes (1936) wrote his *General Theory* in response to the events of that time and he made fundamental uncertainty, as described above, an essential part of his theory. That aspect of Keynes' thinking was widely forgotten, even by those who claimed to be Keynes' successors (e.g. Malinvaud, 1980; Mankiw, 1989). However, consideration of how to deal with situations of uncertainty (as opposed to risk) is at the core of Keynesian economics (Skidelsky, 2010).

In this regard, anti-cyclical fiscal policy is more than just a mechanical tool to stimulate or restrain the economy in times of slack or boom. Rather, it serves to limit fundamental uncertainty of private agents by promising a decisive credibly counteracting state. In time of deep depression the prospect of public demand helps sustain optimism in businesses, while the prospect of fiscal restriction promotes business caution in times of economic euphoria.

Beyond differing in many details, mainstream economics models also generally assumed that markets are inherently stable (Lucas, 1979). Consequently, even the probabilistic risks they included could not endanger stability. Their arguments were twofold. One argument was that flexibility of prices of wages would ensure market clearing, with price adjustment ensuring the economy would move in the right direction to balance supply and demand at desired levels. Mainstream models differ in the speed of price and wage adjustment (Skidelsky, 2010). New Classical models associated with the Chicago School of economics assume a very high speed of adjustment: neo-Keynesian and new Keynesian models assume a slower speed so that adjustment takes a little longer. In the former, there is basically no need at all for a stabilization policy: in the latter, stabilization policy can play a minor role of speeding-up adjustment. The Washington consensus, named after the location of the IMF, basically adopted a compromise between New Classical and New Keynesian thinking (Gali and Gertler, 1999; Gali and Gertler, 2007).

The second argument concerns the rationality of economic agents, who are assumed to know that the model is stable, therefore expect it to be stable via by rational expectations, and thereby make it stable (Barro, 1976; Sargent, 2008). This self-fulfilling rationality reasoning significantly strengthens the stability of the model because shocks are perceived as temporary distortions that provide no reason to panic. Agents simply assume the economy eventually returns to equilibrium with fully employed capacities and full employment, and that assumption prevents panic-stricken behavior, thereby rendering the economy stable.

Furthermore, rational expectations speed up the adjustment process, which further diminishes the need for stabilization policy. If everybody expects to return to stability, there is no incentive to reduce consumption or investment significantly. Moreover, if prices only adjust slowly, there is a strong incentive to increase demand now since prices may be higher after return to equilibrium. Hence, rational expectations strengthen stability and accelerate the adjustment process.

It is absolutely clear that the financial markets and the macro economy are not governed by this type of mechanism. During the financial crisis agents panicked. They either did not believe in the inherent stability of the private sector or they did not have rational expectations. The result is the same: instability. Suddenly, and in complete contradiction to the conclusions of mainstream economic thinking, there was need for massive public intervention to ensure a return to a stable equilibrium (Horn et al., 2010).

This makes clear that an urgent task in a renewed economic thinking is to find a better way to deal with uncertainty (Skidelsky, 2010). There are several ways of meeting this challenge. The first is to change the way expectations are formed. One option is bounded rationality whereby even if the economy is stable, people may not know it. The reasons for bounded rationality are many: they include lack of knowledge and high costs of information collection. People also need to learn how the economy works. That takes time and during the learning period they cannot by definition have rational expectations (Evans and Honkapohja, 2001). Heterogeneous expectation concepts also lead to different policy implications compared to the standard New Classical Model. Even if only a fraction of people lack rational expectations, the implication is a significantly slower adjustment process that gives leeway for positive effects from stabilization policy. Since people clearly are heterogeneous, that provides another reason for future economists to give up the assumption of uniform rational expectations in macroeconomic models.

Economic history shows that economies, especially financial markets, have repeatedly developed bubbles and epochs of irrational exuberance (Lux, 1995). Future models should therefore include assumptions that permit such developments. Herd behavior against the backdrop of uncertainty can easily produce instability. When nobody knows or understands what is happening, people follow the behavior of a seemingly knowing person or institution. But if all head into the same direction, overshooting is inevitable. In that case, panic may develop quickly, triggering deteriorating effects on the whole economy. Even rational expectations would allow for instability in this setting as a rational person would go with the herd once it is on the move. Rational expectations may therefore even accelerate an unstable process.

Plurality of thinking

The almost complete failure of modern macro economics has an even a deeper root than just benign neglect of uncertainty. That failure is dogmatism and lack of pluralism. Lucas (1980) postulated that economic research should only focus on micro-foundations, even when the object of research is the macro economy. The combination of neoclassical microeconomics and the assumption that people act rationally, leaves little room for macroeconomic policy. Instead, macroeconomic policy becomes a potential major source of economic distortion, which explains why mainstream economists have advocated a rather passive state.

There is no problem with the micro-foundations research program *per se*. It is interesting to know what part of macroeconomic phenomena is caused by microeconomic phenomena such as wrong incentives. However, problems arise when microeconomics is seen as the only reasonable way to approach macroeconomics. That has been the case in many faculties, universities and in economic policy for the last three decades, and it has been especially damaging as regards economic policy.

The basic problem is that following just one line of thinking entails high risk. What if that line of thinking proves incomplete or even wrong? In academics the damage is just loss of reputation. In economic policy an entire economy can suffer via loss of jobs and growth. With respect to economic policy advice, it is always advisable to allow for several lines of thinking before taking a decision. Plurality of thought is an essential feature of good policy making. Viewed in that light, economics has to become more Keynesian again as part of reconstructing pluralism in thinking (Skidelsky, 2010).

This advice of plurality of thought in policymaking has not been followed for the past two decades. In Germany, and to a lesser degree in the US, there has been an almost monolithic culture rooted in the so-called "Washington consensus". The result of this monoculture was the financial crisis and Great Recession. The advice for future economic policy makers is: never trust just one economic theory.

Macro-foundations of micro economics

Interestingly the first signs of a major change in macroeconomic thinking started long before the Great recession. There have always been alternatives to the mainstream, such as Old Keynesian and Post Keynesian economics.

However, these alternatives were marginalized in economic debates and not seen as relevant or intellectually important.

Against that backdrop, behavioral economics has emerged and it also provides results that are clearly not in line with prevailing microeconomic theory and macroeconomic models (Duffy, 2008). In particular, the kind of microeconomic rationality applied in mainstream macroeconomic models is not corroborated by many behavioral economics experiments. Instead, it turns out that many people follow social norms in their microeconomic behavior (Akerlof, 2007). People simply do not do certain things although they may be economically rational because society or peer groups will not accept them (Fehr and Goette, 2003). Contrary to standard models, loss of reputation and one's sense of own identity may provide stronger incentives to behave in a certain manner than simple monetary incentives.

This reasoning about the role of norms leads to an almost revolutionary conclusion. It may be sensible to research the macro-foundations of microeconomics rather than - as in recent times - the other way round.

That would fit into an already a longer existing line of research that makes heterogeneity an issue (Ball and Cecchetti, 1988). If people are different, meaning they differ in their preferences, their information sets, and the way they form their expectations, it becomes difficult to find an equilibrium in which all transactions are coordinated at desired levels. This is because under such circumstances it is impossible to anticipate how other market participants will react to changes in demand patterns. This is especially important in times of crisis when uncertainty is already high due to difficult economic conditions. Uncertainty resulting from heterogenity only compounds this, making the private sector even more unstable.

From a macroeconomic perspective it is rational to establish societal norms governing how people should behave in certain situations. Such norms provide agents with better information on how others will act and react. In this fashion, norms may stabilize the economy.

In sum, improved access to information and stabilizing norms can increase an economy's resilience and reduce the likelihood of an economy overshooting in any direction. That suggests future economists should devote research effort to exploring the role of norms for individual behavior and the impact of norms on macroeconomic performance.

The necessity of a political economics

Looking across all the lines of research a future economist should address, one arrives at an important conclusion. Economics should be seen and understood as political science. This should not be interpreted as a request that economics be more closely linked to party politics. Rather, it is necessary that economics take account of the society it is addressing. Political and sociological conditions can vary significantly across economies. Economics should develop methods for including that in its models. Doing so requires that economics puts more emphasis on macroeconomics, not as a derivative of microeconomics, but in its own right. It implies that respective macroeconomic conditions must be taken into account. In particular, it must address the question of how to stabilize the inherent instability of the private sector. Above all, it must not be forgotten that economics always deals with uncertainty, a situation in which probability theory is inapplicable so that conventional statistics is of no help. Addressing this conundrum will require methodological improvement.

If future economists take account of the above considerations, they should be able to give sound policy advice. That does not mean that economists will all give the same advice. Debate will always be an important part of economics. But in the future, hopefully, economics will recognize that political considerations constitute an important part of economic thinking.

References

Akerlof, G. (2007), "The Missing Motivation", Presidential Address for the American economic Association, manuscript, download: http://www.aeaweb.org/annual_mtg_papers/2007/0106_1640_0101.pdf 2007.

Ball, L. and Cecchetti, S. G. (1988), "Imperfect Information and Staggered Price Setting", *American Economic Review*, vol.78, pp 999 - 1018.

Barro, R. A. (1976), "Rational Expectations and the Role of Monetary Policy", *Journal of Monetary Policy*, vol 1.

Clarida R., Gali, J., and Gertler, M. (1999), "The Science of Monetary Policy: A New Keynesian Perspective", *Journal of Economic Literature*, vol. XXXVII, pp1661-1707.

Colander,D., Föllmer,H., Haas,A., Goldberg, M., Juselius, K., Kirman, A., Lux, T., and Sloth, B. (2009), "The Financial Crisis and the Systemic Failure of Academic Economics", University of Copenhagen, Discussion Papers 09-03.

De Grauwe , P. and Ji, Y. (2012), "Mispricing of Sovereign Risks and Multiple Equilibria in the Eurozone", CEPs Working Paper No. 361, January.

Duffy, J. (2008), "Macroeconomics: A Survey of Laboratory Research", manuscript, March, download: http://www.pitt.edu/~jduffy/papers/hee11.pdf.

Evans, G. W. and Honkapohja, S. (2001), "Expectations and the Stability Problem for Optimal Monetary Policies", CEPR Discussion Papers No. 2805, June 2001.

Fehr E. and Goette, L. (2003), "Robustness and Real Consequences of Nominal Wage Rigidity", Institute for Empirical Research in Economics, University of Zurich, Working Paper No.44.

Gali, J. and Gertler, M. (2007), "Macroeconomic Modeling for Monetary Policy Evaluation", *Journal of Economic Perspectives*, American Economic Association, vol. 21(4), pages 25-46, Fall.

Horn, G. A., Sturn, S. , Tober, S., and Truger, A. (2010), "Herausforderungen für die Wirtschaftspolitik 2010. Geldpolitik, Finanzpolitik und Arbeitsmarktpolitik in diesem Jahr". IMK Report Nr. 46, January.

IMK, OFCE, and WIFO (2013), "Crisis continues to smoulder", IMK Report Nr. 80e, Mai 2013, Joint analysis of the Macro Group IMK (Düsseldorf), OFCE (Paris) und WIFO (Wien).

Keynes, J. M. (1936), *The General Theory of Employment, Interest and Money*, (C.W., Vol. XII).

Lucas, R. E. jr (1979), "An Equilibrium Model of the Business Cycle", *Journal of Political Economy*, 83, pp 113-144.

Lucas, R. E. jr. (1980), "Methods and Problems in the Business Cycle Theory", *Journal of Money, Credit and Banking*, vol 12, pp 696-715.

Lux ,T. (1995), "Herd Behaviour, Bubbles and Crashes", *Economic Journal*, vol .105, pp 881-896.

Malinvaud, E. (1980), *Profitability and Unemployment*, Cambridge University Press.

Mankiw, N. G. (1989), "Real Business Cycle: A New Keynesian Perspective", *Journal of Economic Perspectives*, vol.3, No.3, pp 79-90.

Sargent, T. (2008), "Evolution and Intelligent Design", *American Economic Review*, vol. 98:1, pp 5-37.

Skidelsky, R. (2010), Die Rückkehr des Meisters, Kunstmann, München.

II
Keynesian Economics Versus Austerity

5. The Great Mistake: How Academic Economists and Policymakers Wrongly Abandoned Fiscal Policy

Josh Bivens, *Ph.D., Director of Research, Economic Policy Institute, Washington, DC*
lbivens@epi.org

Introduction: an unacceptably slow recovery

As of the middle of 2013, the US economy remained far from fully recovered from the effects of the Great Recession. The "output gap" between actual GDP and potential GDP – how much could have been produced had unemployment and capacity utilization not been depressed due to insufficient aggregate demand – stood at 5.8 percent of potential GDP, or roughly $900 billion. This is by far the largest output gap measured in terms of time from either the previous business cycle peak or the trough of the recession. Furthermore, the cumulative lost output since the beginning of the Great Recession is nearly double the amount lost during any other recession since the Great Depression (and will in coming years surely rise to more than double any other previous losses). Perhaps worst of all, this gap had barely changed in the previous two years – shrinking by only 0.5 percent of GDP since the beginning of 2011.

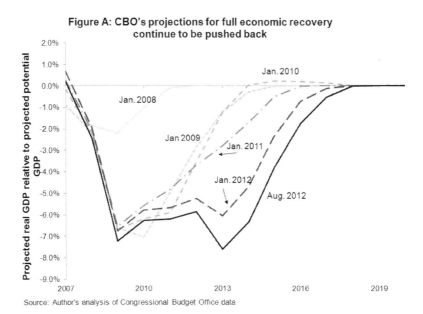

Figure A: CBO's projections for full economic recovery continue to be pushed back

Source: Author's analysis of Congressional Budget Office data

The stubbornly slow progress of recovery has consistently surprised policymakers. This is captured in Figure A which shows the projected course of recovery as forecast by successive iterations of the Congressional Budget Office's (CBO) Budget and Economic Outlooks.

Macroeconomic roots and context of the Great Recession call for fiscal response

However, the roots of this slow recovery are far from mysterious: the very large negative shock to aggregate demand provided by the bursting housing bubble (starting in 2007) has never been fully neutralized by policy measures to boost demand. Moreover, because the housing bubble burst in a macroeconomic environment characterized by already low interest rates and inflation, monetary policymakers quickly found themselves hard up against the zero lower bound on the nominal "policy" interest rates controlled by the Federal Reserve. This made conventional counter-cyclical monetary policy ineffective, a state of play that is often referred to as a "liquidity trap".

Liquidity trap conditions argue strongly that expansionary fiscal policy should be the primary tool used to spur recovery. However, fiscal policy as a macroeconomic stabilization tool had fallen deeply out of favor among many academic macroeconomists in recent decades – and had reached the depths of disfavor immediately preceding the Great Recession. This degree of disfavor is tellingly captured by the fact that the most rousing defense offered by an influential academic in the 2000s was not titled "The Case For Discretionary Fiscal Policy", but rather "The Case Against the Case Against Discretionary Fiscal Policy".

Normal arguments against fiscal stabilization invalid during Great Recession

The "case against discretionary fiscal policy" rests on two arguments: first, the possibility of interest rate "crowding-out" that keeps fiscal multipliers close to zero, and second the possibility that expenditure timing lags would cause any discretionary fiscal impulse to come too late and actually make policy pro-cyclical.

The "crowding out" argument simply states that by increasing its borrowing, the federal government is competing with private sector borrowers for loanable funds. This increased competition may well raise overall interest rates, and some private sector borrowers may decide at these higher rates to not engage in the investment or consumption project they would have engaged in at lower rates. Hence, the extra activity spurred by fiscal policy "crowds out" some degree of private-sector activity by pushing up interest rates. In the extreme, this crowding-out can be complete, leading to no increase at all in economic activity stemming from large increases in fiscal support.[1] A second cause of crowding out can result from the central bank's "reaction function" which may respond to increased fiscal support by making monetary policy less expansionary.

The mistiming case against discretionary fiscal policy stabilizations holds that fiscal policy support is often associated with lags both in deliberation (the inside lag) as well as implementation (the outside lag). These lags imply that that fiscal policy support may be injected into the economy after an economic recovery has already (spontaneously) begun. Because monetary policy tends to operate with a much-shorter inside lag, recent decades had seen a growing (but not universal) agreement among policymakers and macroeconomists that most recession-fighting responsibilities should be borne by the Federal Reserve, and not by Congress and the President.[2]

Neither of these two arguments against discretionary fiscal policy applied to the Great Recession. Worries that budget deficits would sharply boost interest rates, choking off spending and neutralizing any fiscal impulse, were particularly misplaced. The demand shock spurred by the housing bubble's burst was so large that national savings far exceeded desired investment at positive interest rates, meaning that there was ferocious downward pressure on interest rates. And the Federal Reserve also made clear that it would not try to neutralize expansionary fiscal policy measures by raising its short-term policy interest rate. In fact, it even promised to support expansionary fiscal policy by undertaking unconventional measures to lower longer-term interest rates through large-scale asset purchases.

Ironically, as regards timing, the case against discretionary fiscal stabilizations seems to have won greatest agreement among policymakers and economists just as the argument was losing much of its force. Between 1947 and 1990, recessions were indeed quite short and recoveries tended to follow rapidly after business cycle troughs. However, beginning in 1981, it has taken progressively longer for recoveries to generate anything close to full resource utilization. Thus, the last three recessions – even those with a relatively mild depth (like in 2001) – only saw full recovery of employment years after the official recession ended.

---

[1] This presentation is the closed-economy version of crowding out. It should also be noted that in models with a fixed global interest rate, fiscal support can be crowded-out by a one-for-one decrease in net exports stemming from a strengthening of the national currency's value that follows the increased fiscal support.

[2] Blinder (2004) outlines the timing arguments in some detail. Probably the most famous statement of how countercyclical interventions have the potential to increase economic instability comes from Friedman (1953).

The "Keynesian Moment" of 2008/9 proves too short

During the downturn phase of the Great Recession, as job-losses reached a staggering 750,000 per month, this bias against discretionary fiscal stabilization was relaxed. This created a temporary "Keynesian Moment" in policymaking, which it reached its apogee with the passage of the American Recovery and Reinvestment Act (ARRA) in early 2009. This moment is clearly captured in Figure B which shows growth in real federal government expenditures across post-war recessions. The important feature is the jump in growth of spending five quarters after the beginning of the 2007 recession.

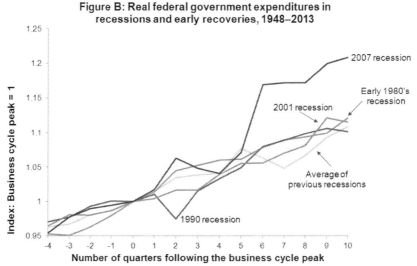

Figure B: Real federal government expenditures in recessions and early recoveries, 1948–2013

Note: The average of all previous recessions is the average of government expenditures for the six recessions and subsequent recoveries between 1948-1980. The early 1980's recession begins in 1980Q1 and spans through 1982Q4 to cover the recession from 1980Q1-1980Q3 and the subsequent recession from 1981Q3 through 1982Q4.. The start of the recovery begins in 1982 Q4.
Source: Author's analysis of Federal Reserve Board Federal Reserve Economic Data public data series

This burst of fiscal activism halted the economy's free-fall by mid-2009, and even created demand growth sufficient to push down measured unemployment by late 2010. However, the Keynesian moment was clearly too short.

The ARRA provided a fiscal boost that was both temporary and left the economy well short of full-employment. Recognizing this, the Obama administration also made efforts to keep fiscal policy from whipsawing sharply negative in 2011 and 2012, even to the extent of delaying long-standing priorities like rolling back the Bush-era tax cuts for high-income in exchange for some measures of fiscal support (notably, the 2 percent temporary payroll tax cut in 2011 and 2012).

But even with these efforts, fiscal policy since the official end of the Great Recession (in June 2009) has been sharply contractionary when compared with historical averages, particularly once one factors in state and local expenditures. Figure C below extends the measures of real government (federal and state/local this time) spending past the official end of recessions and into the subsequent recovery periods. It shows that fiscal policy has been much weaker in the 2007 recession than in prior recessions.

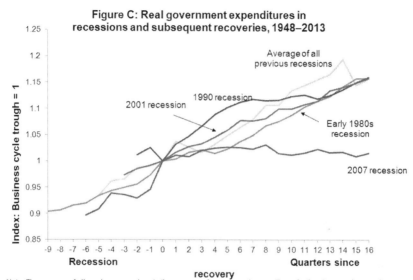

Figure C: Real government expenditures in recessions and subsequent recoveries, 1948–2013

Note: The average of all previous recessions is the average of government expenditures for the six recessions and subsequent recoveries between 1948-1980. The early 1980's recession begins in 1980Q1 and spans through 1982Q4 to cover the recession from 1980Q1-1980Q3 and the subsequent recession from 1981Q3 through 1982Q4. The start of the recovery begins in 1982 Q4.
Source: Author's analysis of Bureau of Economic Analysis *National Income and Product Acounts* (Table 3.1)

The most striking comparison is with the recovery following the steep recession of the early 1980s. The output gap at the trough of the early 1980s recession was actually larger than that at the trough of the Great Recession, yet two years following that trough 80 percent of the output gap had been erased. In contrast, four years after the trough of the Great Recession less than 20 percent of the output gap has been erased.

Furthermore, the scope for monetary policy to boost recovery was far larger in the early 1980s recession as the Federal Reserve was able to lower the federal funds rate by almost 10 percentage points. This was not possible in the Great Recession, and it means there should have been even larger compensating fiscal stimulus.

Given the similar size of output gaps at the trough of these two recessions and given that the Federal Reserve was able to do more to counter the 1980 recession, it is axiomatic that a larger fiscal expansion was needed after the end of the Great Recession to sustain recovery. Instead, real government spending four years into recovery is approximately 15 percent below what it would be had it just it matched average government spending patterns in prior recoveries. The result has been tragic. Had these average patterns been replicated in the current recovery, roughly 90 percent of today's output gap would have been closed.

There is an important lesson here. Calls to address the jobs-crisis with a fiscal boost commensurate to the scale of the problem are often greeted by implicit claims that this would constitute wild and historically unprecedented degree of public spending. That is not so. The US economy has implemented such fiscal support for prior recoveries, including the recent past. There is nothing either economically or historically "unrealistic" about the calls for such fiscal stimulus now. If enacted, ending austerity and returning to past fiscal stimulus patterns would end the jobs-crisis.

Winning the intellectual debate but losing the policy debate on austerity

Among academic macroeconomists, the debate over the merits of austerity versus stimulus as a precondition to pushing economies back to full-employment was largely over by the end of 2012, with austerity the clear loser.

The most-visible manifestation of austerity's intellectual defeat is captured in a paper by Herndon, Ash, and Pollin (2013, HAP). Their paper exposed the extreme weakness of the claim put forward by Reinhart and Rogoff (2010, R&R) that economic growth falls off a cliff once public debt to GDP ratios exceed 90 percent. Building on earlier work by Bivens and Irons (2010), HAP showed that the R&R result was wholly driven by a combination of inappropriate (and oddly idiosyncratic) methods for weighting country/year episodes of high debt plus a sample selection that simply omitted country/debt episodes that weakened their results. The tragedy is that the R&R paper was initially extremely influential in the stimulus policy debate, providing a result that fed the intellectual bias against fiscal policy that had developed over the past thirty years.

Further evidence on the damage wrought by austerity has been provided in a working paper, co-authored by the chief economist of the International Monetary Fund (IMF), and released in late 2012. That paper showed growth forecast errors were consistently related to the degree of fiscal consolidation undertaken by countries in recent years (with greater consolidation correlating with larger negative growth forecast errors).[3] Since the IMF was already assuming moderate damage to growth from fiscal consolidation (information embedded in growth forecasts), this finding was interpreted as strong evidence that fiscal multipliers were consistently larger than had previously been estimated.

US not the E.U., yet

The most compelling evidence regarding the toll of austerity in recent years comes from the experience of the Eurozone countries – particularly the periphery countries of Spain, Greece, and Portugal. Eurozone unemployment has remained over 12 percent in the second half of 2013, up from the 7.5 overall percent rate that prevailed before the start of the Great Recession. This is despite the fact that Germany, which is Europe's largest economy and accounts for more than a quarter of total Eurozone output, has had a strong employment recovery. Moreover, Eurozone unemployment has worsened markedly since the beginning of 2010, whereas the US has seen some improvement.

The source of this difference in US – Eurozone performance is not mysterious. Though government spending slowed in the United States, there was no turn to outright austerity such as occurred in the Eurozone and the United Kingdom. Consequently, US growth and employment has far outpaced growth in Europe. Of course, it could have been even better had the US embraced greater fiscal stimulus.

Conclusion

The bitter irony is that even as the intellectual case for austerity has crumbled, the politics of austerity have prevailed so that policy has begun ratchet up austerity in 2013. Unless there is a rapid change, US policy is now on a trajectory that will see US fiscal policy increasingly resemble the UK and Eurozone in coming years. The Obama administration was able to avoid the turn to outright austerity for a couple of years after the ARRA's spending petered out. However, the very large budget cuts demanded by House Republicans in exchange for raising the legislative debt ceiling in August 2011 took effect at the beginning of 2013 (epitomized by the now-infamous "sequester" cuts) and will persist in coming years.

---

[3] Blanchard, Olivier and Daniel Leigh (2013), "Growth forecast errors and fiscal multipliers", IMF Working Paper. The key finding of this paper was previewed, however, in the September 2012 World Economic Outlook.

The failure to allow fiscal support to match that provided during past economic recoveries was a serious error on the part of macroeconomic policymakers. That error is now being compounded.

As for professional macroeconomists, their widespread agreement prior to the crisis on the irrelevance of fiscal policy for macroeconomic stabilization looks in hindsight to be a major intellectual blunder. Unfortunately, because ideas change slowly it continues to have massive damaging consequences. In light of the crisis, this view of fiscal policy irrelevance should be high on the list of economic dogmas to be discarded.

References

Blanchard, Olivier and Daniel Leigh (2013), "Growth forecast errors and fiscal multipliers", IMF Working Paper. International Monetary Fund.

Bivens, Josh and John Irons (2010), "Government debt and economic growth". Briefing Paper #271. Economic Policy Institute. Washington, DC.

Blinder, Alan (2004), "The case against the case against discretionary fiscal policy". Center for Economic Policy Studies Working Paper 100, Princeton University.

Friedman, Milton (1953), "The effects of a full-employment policy on economic stability: A formal analysis", in M. Friedman, *Essays in Positive Economics*. Chicago: University of Chicago Press.

Herndon, Thomas, Michael Ash and Robert Pollin (2013), "Does high public debt consistently stifle economic growth? A critique of Reinhart and Rogoff." Working Paper. Political Economy Research Institute. University of Massachusetts-Amherst.

6. Mental Barriers to Macroeconomic Policy Making: The Sad State of (German) Mainstream Economics[1]

Achim Truger, *Professor of Economics, Berlin School of Economics and Law, Berlin, Germany, Achim.Truger@hwr-berlin.de.*

Introduction

The most important problem with macroeconomic policy making at the moment is not a lack of progressive Keynesian proposals, it is a lack of implementation. Instead of learning the obvious lessons from the Great Recession and abandoning much of the pre-crisis economic policy consensus framed by the so called New Consensus Macroeconomics, politicians all over the world have embarked on regressive austerity policies.

Arguably, the current situation in the European Union is the most dramatic as the radical austerity measures forced upon the periphery countries have led to deep economic depressions with record levels of unemployment and corresponding severe economic and social hardship for the population. Furthermore, this is not just a short-term reaction. Instead, the institutional foundations of austerity policies have been strongly reinforced by 'reforms' of the Stability and Growth Pact and the introduction of 'constitutional debt brakes' in many EU countries by the 'Fiscal Compact' (European Council 2012).

What is hard to understand is the lack of economic justification and the fact that the devastating consequences of the austerity policies were completely predictable, even from a mainstream view. Simply applying standard fiscal multiplier estimates (see Heming et al., 2002; Bouthevillain et al., 2009; and Gechert and Will, 2012) to the huge size of the austerity packages, sometimes in the range of more than 10 per cent of GDP in just a few years (OECD 2012), meant austerity would be devastating.

This brief essay focuses on one potential explanation for the absence of sensible macroeconomic policies starting from Keynes's famous dictum that '[...] the ideas of economists and political philosophers, both when they are right and when they are wrong, are more powerful than is commonly understood. Indeed the world is ruled by little else.'(Keynes 1936: 383). If Keynes was right then the main problem would be that politicians or more generally the public discourse today are simply dominated by the wrong ideas.

---

[1] This article draws on ideas and material developed in more detail and in a broader context in Truger (2013).

In that sense it is important to trace those mental barriers to macroeconomic policy making and see where they come from.

This essay argues that the mental barriers are very strong in Germany as the most economically and politically influential member state of the Euro area (section 2), and the essay tries to show, with the help of an example, how stubbornly anti-Keynesian most academic economists in Germany are (section 3). If the diagnosis is right, part of the solution to Europe's economic problems will be efforts to change the German economic discourse and encourage and strengthen less orthodox academic economists in Germany (section 4).

German dogmatism vs. American pragmatism in macroeconomic policy?

As is well known, Germany and especially the German Bundesbank's monetarist/new-classical ideas, have significantly influenced the institutional set-up of the European Monetary Union. This is confirmed with undisguised pride by Hans Tietmeyer (2005), former president of the German Bundesbank. However, in the rest of the world this raised some doubts regarding the rather special ideas dominating Germany's position towards macroeconomic policies. In 1999 Paul Krugman tried to trace the origins of that narrow mind-set in one of his op-eds in the *New York Times* entitled "Why Germany kant kompete." He argued that the main difference between the German and the US approach may not be political but philosophical:

> 'The real divide [...] is not political but philosophical; it's not Karl Marx vs. Adam Smith, it's Immanuel Kant's categorical imperative vs. William James' pragmatism. What the Germans really want is a clear set of principles: rules that specify the nature of truth, the basis of morality, when shops will be open, and what a Deutsche mark is worth. [...] in an environment where deflation is more of a threat than inflation, an obsession with sound money can be a recipe for permanent recession.' (Krugman 1999)

When Germany was facing serious economic troubles in the first half of first decade of the new century that it tried to solve by austerity and labour market reforms, Robert Solow commented on the narrowness of the economic policy discussion in German expert circles:

> "All I want to do, as an outside observer, is to call attention to the extremely and unnecessarily narrow focus of the current discussion of macro-policy in expert circles in Germany. It is not too much to say, in my view, that there is almost no proper discussion of

specifically macroeconomic problems and remedies. Instead, there is always talk of labor-market reform [...]. These are important issues, and reforms are surely desirable. But stopping with them is exactly what I mean by a narrow focus and an evasion of macroeconomic factors. I think that this limitation is symptomatic of a misunderstanding of both the German situation and macroeconomic theory. (Solow 2008: 20)"

Finally, when the Euro crisis escalated in 2010, Wolfgang Münchau wrote in the *Financial Times* on 17 November 2010 that the sheer degree of incompetence at the top level of the German government was breath-taking. In fact, German officials acted as if they deliberately wanted to worsen the crisis with their reluctance and their insistence on so-called sound economic principles, when it should have been clear that sticking to those principles would cause economic disaster. Later on, two leading German central bankers, Axel Weber, the president of the Bundesbank, and Jürgen Stark, the chief economist of the ECB, resigned from their posts, because they opposed the ECB's buying government bonds in the secondary market of countries currently in trouble.

The 'Hamburg appeal' as a stunning example of German economist's stubborn anti-Keynesianism

According to Keynes' dictum quoted above, one should not necessarily assume vested interest behind the behaviour of German politicians. Instead, one should assume that they believe in what they are doing, and one should therefore realize that a vast majority of the German economics profession supplied them with and supported them in their views. One of the most spectacular examples of the narrowness of the German debate is the 'Hamburger Appell' ('Hamburg Appeal') in 2005 (Funke et al. 2005). In this appeal more than 250 German university professors of economics[2] – many of them prominent – collectively addressed the public in a pre-election appeal aimed at preventing German economic policy from taking demand-side measures and insisting instead on labour market deregulation, dismantling the welfare state, and fiscal austerity that had been boosted in 2003. The professors started their appeal with the following introduction:

"The economic policy debate in Germany is increasingly being coined by conceptions that show an alarming lack of economic

---

[2] The complete list of signatories can be accessed via the following link:
http://www.wiso.uni-hamburg.de/professuren/wachstum-und-konjunktur/hamburger-appell/unterzeichner/

expertise. This is all the more reason for concern as Germany is in the midst of a deep structural crisis that calls for drastic and painful reforms. Precisely in pre-election times the willingness to bring this fact home to citizens with the necessary clarity will be small. Instead of that, important politicians yield to the temptation of propagating concepts that are not scientifically founded and aim at combining the agreeable with the useful: By adequate measures, it is suggested, an increase in domestic demand could be achieved, thereby leading to an overcoming of the structural growth crisis. This idea is wrong and dangerous. As academic teachers of economics we vividly caution against producing illusions thereby undermining the acceptance of necessary reforms. We appeal to the elected representatives' sense of responsibility to resist the temptation of easy solutions and to instead give non-sugarcoated answers to the pressing economic questions. (Funke et al. 2005: 1; translation by the author)"

The professors were obviously very explicit in their rejection of any demand side measures and, according to their view, they were not just stating their opinion. They also denounced other opinions as wrong and not scientifically founded. They invoked all their authority as scientists by referring to their status as academic teachers of economics. Turning specifically to fiscal policy matters they stated:

"The uncontrollably growing German government debt is quite correctly being perceived as future tax burden. [...] Therefore, anybody who undermines the incentives to consolidate the government debt on the national or international level will damage the German interest. Any expansion of government debt will weaken domestic demand, because structural imbalances will be reinforced instead of cured, so that citizens and firms will have to act with increased caution. The (mass) purchasing power argument against "saving oneself to death" in times of economic stagnation may be convenient, however, it is wrong. [...] Therefore, responsible fiscal policy must be strictly stability oriented. The consolidation of government finances calls for far reaching cuts in all areas of public spending. [...] Anybody claiming anything to the contrary will not do justice to the economic challenges for Germany or he will mislead citizens in a populist manner. (Funke et al. 2005: 2; translation by the author)"

From a theoretical point of view, what is most remarkable about this quote is that it claims that any increase in the government deficit will actually lead to a decrease in demand. The theoretical reasons given for this claim are few and weak. Basically, the only way to justify the German professors' claims is to involve non-Keynesian effects. The mentioning of the perception of public debt as future tax burden is a clear hint in this direction. However, the case for the dominance of non-Keynesian effects is difficult to make, and yet the professors make it sound as if any other possibility were unscientific.

Of course, non-Keynesian effects were intensely discussed at the time, but they were not as uncontroversial as (implicitly) postulated by the German professors. By 2005 non-Keynesian effects had made their way into the standard macroeconomic textbooks. However, they were certainly not referred to as the normal or standard - let alone the only case - but as a theoretical possibility that may become important empirically under certain rather narrow conditions (see e.g. Blanchard 2003: 364). Furthermore, the German professors ignored three empirical studies investigating the existence of non-Keynesian effects for the specific German case (Leibfritz et al. 2001; SVR 2003; Plötscher et al. 2005). All of them concluded that in the short run Keynesian effects dominate in Germany, providing a clear refutation of the German professors' assertion.

The last way out of this embarrassing situation may be to deny that there were any demand side problems in Germany at the time of the appeal in 2005. However, according to all existing estimates the output gap of the German economy was substantially negative in 2005. Therefore, it must be concluded that the 250 professors – although invoking their authority as academic teachers – were in fact giving advice that was plainly in contradiction to both standard textbook knowledge and to the available empirical studies.

Obviously, if such a large and important fraction of a country's academic economists can publicly deviate from basic academic standards without any major critical discussion and objection, this is an indication of severe mental barriers to even modestly sensible macroeconomic policies.

How to overcome the mental barriers against sensible macroeconomic policies in Germany?

The above argument is open to criticism. First, one may want to argue against Keynes' famous dictum claiming that, in fact, vested interest is a much more important determinant of economic policy than economic ideas. However, this is hard to reconcile with the facts. It is difficult to see how Germany, or indeed major economic players in Germany, would gain by depressing its own domestic demand given the stagnant nature of economic conditions between 2001 and 2005. Nor would Germany gain by depressing the economies of its most important trading partners within the Euro area in the current Euro crisis. Such policy only makes sense if one believes in ideas derived from neoclassical/monetarist/new-classical/new-consensus   austerity   type   of reasoning.

Second, one may want to question whether the quoted 2005 'Hamburg appeal' has ever or still captures the mind-set of German mainstream economists. However, although some progress is discernible in recent discussions, a collective progressive declaration in another direction is still missing. Where is a major collective declaration of German economists warning against the economic and social problems of austerity, that economists in other European countries have initiated?

To conclude, if the above diagnosis is true, then part of the solution to Europe's economic problems will be efforts to change German economic discourse so as to encourage and strengthen academic pluralism and less orthodox economists in Germany. Economists from abroad, and especially the US, have a major role to play in publicly questioning German economic wisdom and convincing the German public and politicians of more sensible economic policies for Germany and Europe.

References

Blanchard, O. (2003): *Macroeconomics*, 3rd ed., Upper Saddle River, NJ et al.: Prentice Hall.

Bouthevillain. C. et al (2009): Pros and cons of various fiscal measures to stimulate the economy, *Banco de Espana Economic Bulletin*, July 2009, 123-144.

European Council (2012): Treaty on Stability, Coordination and Governance in the Economic and Monetary Union, 2 March 2012, Brussels, European Council, (http://european-council.europa.eu/eurozone-governance/treaty-on-stability?lang=en)

Funke, M., Lucke, B., Straubhaar, T. (2005): Hamburger Appell, (http://www.wiso.uni-hamburg.de/fileadmin/wiso_vwl_iwk/paper/appell.pdf).

Gechert, S., Will, H. (2012): Fiscal Multipliers: A Meta-Regression Analysis, Institut für Makroökonomie und Konjunkturforschung, Working Paper No. 97, Düsseldorf.

Hemming, R., Kell, M. and Mahfouz, S. (2002): The Effectiveness of Fiscal Policy in Stimulating Economic Activity: A Review of the Literature, International Monetary Fund Working Paper No. 02/208, Washington DC

Keynes, J.M. (1936): *The General Theory of Employment Interest and Money*, London: Palgrave Macmillan (reprinted 2007).

Krugman, P. (1999): Why Germany kant kompete, (http://web.mit.edu/krugman/www/kompete.html).

Leibfritz, W. et al. (2001): Finanzpolitik im Spannungsfeld des Europäischen Stabilitäts- und Wachstumspaktes. Zwischen gesamtwirtschaftlichen Erfordernissen und wirtschafts- und finanzpolitischem Handlungsbedarf, ifo-Beiträge zur Wirtschaftsforschung 5, München, ifo-Institut für Wirtschaftsforschung.

Plötscher, M., Seidel, T., Westermann, F. (2005): Fiskalpolitik in Deutschland: Eine empirische Analyse am Beispiel des Vorziehens der Steuerreform, Kredit und Kapital, 38 (1), 23-51.

Solow, R. (2008): Broadening the discussion of macroeconomic policy, in: Schettkat, R., Langkau, J. (eds), *Economic Policy Proposals for Germany and Europe*, Milton Park: Routledge, 20-28.

SVR [Sachverständigenrat zur Begutachtung der gesamtwirtschaftlichen Entwicklung] (2003): Jahresgutachten 2003/2004. Staatsfinanzen konsolidieren – Steuersystem reformieren, Wiesbaden: Statistisches Bundesamt.

Tietmeyer, H. (2005): Herausforderung Euro: Wie es zum Euro kam und was er für Deutschlands Zukunft bedeutet, München: Hanser Verlag.

Truger, A. (2013): Austerity in the Euro area: The sad state of economic policy in Germany and the EU, *European Journal of Economics and Economic Policies: Intervention*, 10 (2), forthcoming.

7. Cyclical Doves, Structural Hawks (CDSH): Turning Fiscal Policy Right-Side Up Again

Jared Bernstein, *Senior Fellow, Center on Budget and Policy Priorities, Washington, DC, bernstein@cbpp.org.*

The failure of fiscal austerity

Controlled experiments are rare in economics, and particularly rare in macro. But the last few years have seen a pseudo-experiment of sorts regarding the application of fiscal austerity measures versus Keynesian policies in numerous economies that remain to varying degrees demand constrained. As this and other papers in this volume show, deficit reduction under such conditions has proven to be uniquely unsuccessful in terms of either restoring growth or jobs, or even to reducing debt as a share of Gross Domestic Product (GDP).

And yet, both here and abroad, governments continue to consolidate their debts. Here in the US, we have fiscal headwinds shaving an estimated 1-1.5 points off of real GDP in 2013, the result of the automatic budget cuts ("sequestration") and tax increases, most importantly, the expiration of a payroll tax cut worth 2% to the vast majority of the workforce. In various European economies, as shown below, the countries that consolidated the most had the worst growth outcomes. Moreover, recent International Monetary Fund (IMF) research finds that economists' understanding of these dynamics is quite limited, as forecasters systematically underestimated the extent to which fiscal consolidation would reduce GDP growth.[1]

Why is that? The paper will briefly look at some evidence behind the above claims, and then move into a discussion of how fiscal policy flipped upside down and how those trying to influence the policy process might flip it back. This is important not just in the current context but because there is another downturn lurking out there in our future, and if policy makers fail to learn the lessons embedded in the current moment, they may well get this wrong again next time.

The findings of the paper are as follows:
- Premature fiscal consolidation hurts growth and jobs relative to a counterfactual wherein temporary government support phases out when private sector demand, such as consumption, investment, or an improvement in the current account balance, is solidly back online.

[1] Blanchard and Leigh, 2013. http://www.imf.org/external/pubs/ft/wp/2013/wp1301.pdf

- Yet policy makers, particularly those controlling fiscal policy (less so regarding central bankers plying monetary policy) continue to promote lower budget deficits even in the face of evidence that it is hurting both growth and fiscal conditions.
- These contraindicated behaviors seem to grow out of a large over-estimate of the positive impact of fiscal consolidation on growth as well as on achieving fiscal balance. The US record is particularly clear on the point that strong growth and deficit reduction are complementary, not in conflict.
- Despite all of the above observations, it remains important to recognize that every country faces unique fiscal and financial market challenges. Countries can face spiking bond yields if global investors view them as fiscally reckless. The problem than becomes a serious debt/growth trap, where the interest rate on sovereign debt is higher than the growth rate of nominal GDP.
- At least three political economy factors have contributed to the current misuse of fiscal policy: an over-estimate of the role of the Clinton fiscal policy in achieving surpluses, the "structural dovishness" of the GW Bush years, and the use of deficits as an ideological tool among those whose goal is to severely shrink the size of government.
- I offer a simple framework called "CDSH" to clarify what I believe is a position consistent with effective fiscal policy that expands in bad times and consolidates in bona fide expansions: **C**yclical **D**ove, **S**tructural **H**awk.

Have Austerity Measures Helped?

The term "austerity" has come to mean something quite specific in the current fiscal debates. It is the reduction (often called "consolidation") of government budget deficits, both current and projected, in order to restore consumer and financial market confidence in both the public sector and the broader economy during periods where significant output gaps are present. This new-found confidence is in turn expected to lower any risk premiums on interest rates and thus increase investment, growth and jobs.

If true, we'd expect to see a negative relationship between fiscal consolidation and growth, i.e., as deficits came down, real GDP growth would accelerate. In fact, as this figure from Shambaugh (2012) reveals, a scatterplot (Figure 1, below) of change in government spending and change in real GDP clearly suggests a positive relationship: reduced government spending correlates with slower growth. As Shambaugh puts it[2]:

> "...the early returns suggest that standard economic theory has held all too well. Contractionary fiscal policy is just that: contractionary. The countries undergoing stringent fiscal tightening have faced very slow growth. Further, contraction can wipe out the near-term budget savings as measured by the change in the debt-to-GDP ratio if austerity shrinks GDP by more than it cuts the deficit. In other words, policymakers' attempts to solve the sovereign debt crisis not only may be making the growth crisis worse, but may be making the sovereign debt crisis itself worse as well."

Figure 1. Change in Government Spending and Change in GDP, 2008Q1 to 2011Q1

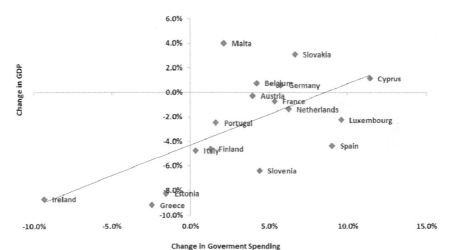

Source: Shambaugh (2012) remade by author (updated Eurostat data and reversed Shambaugh's axes).

Figure 2 focuses on austerity in the Eurozone, plotting real GDP growth and government spending beginning in 2008, both indexed to '1' and with unemployment on the right-hand axis.

---

[2] Shambaugh, 192-3
http://www.brookings.edu/~/media/Projects/BPEA/Spring%202012/2012a_Shambaugh.pdf

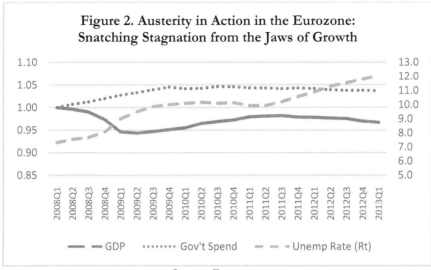

Figure 2. Austerity in Action in the Eurozone: Snatching Stagnation from the Jaws of Growth

Source: Eurostat.

Government spending initially stepped up to offset the sharp contraction of private sector demand, as GDP began to grow and unemployment stabilized. Then, as various governments in the Eurozone prematurely (at least in growth terms) began to consolidate their budget deficits, government spending flattened, unemployment took off again, and GDP reversed course.

Obviously, data like those in the above two figures collapse many moving parts into a simple, if not simplistic, story. Surely, different countries face different pressures. There are cases in southern Eurozone countries where the loss of fiscal credibility is quite clearly linked to very high borrowing costs. Regarding Italy, for example, Corsetti (2012) notes: "The current fiscal tightening is arguably contractionary, but the alternative of not reacting to the credibility loss would have produced much worse consequences." [3]

Such counterfactual reasoning does not, however, explain the adoption of deficit reduction in the UK, nor, for that matter, the US. And while in this country we're on track to stabilize the debt-to-GDP ratio, at least until the pressure of health costs leads the ratio to start growing again (a longer term factor), there are Eurozone countries for whom austerity has been self-defeating even from a fiscal perspective.

To state the obvious, the debt-to-GDP ratio has both a numerator and a denominator. Austerity measures target the numerator (they aim to lower the annual deficits which add to the debt), but also hit the denominator, leading to slower GDP growth as the previous figure reveals. Figure 3 suggests that in the UK and other Organization for Economic Co-Operation and

---

[3] http://www.voxeu.org/article/has-austerity-gone-too-far-new-vox-debate

Development (OECD)countries, as the deficit is falling as a share of GDP in recent years (left panel), the debt is growing.[4]

Figure 3. General Government Deficit and Debt*
as a percentage of GDP

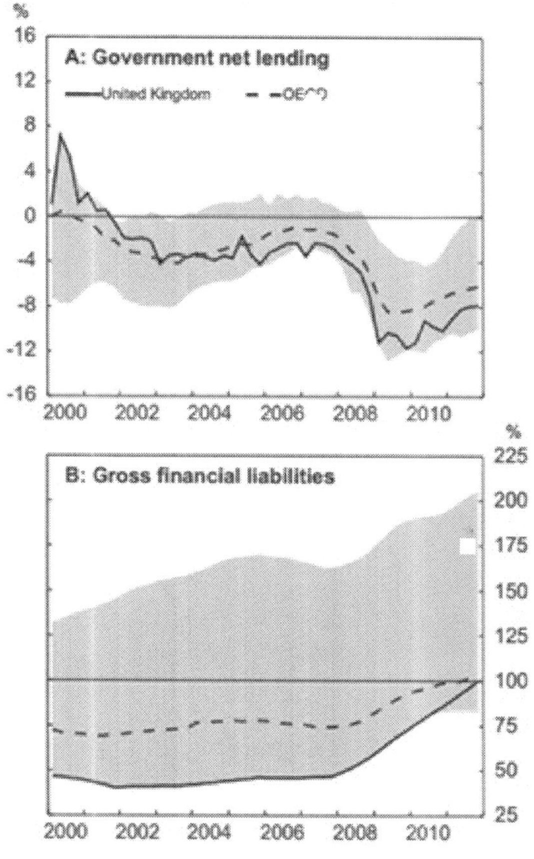

The shaded areas indicate the maximum and the minimum among the seven major OECD countries. Source OEC Economic Outlook 92 database

This evidence is also not a blatant indictment of austerity, because historically large budget deficits, even as they are declining, will typically contribute to higher debt-to-GDP ratios. It is only when the budget comes into primary balance—when government receipts are large enough to pay all annual costs other than interest payments—that the debt ratio will stabilize.

---

[4] OECD, http://www.oecd.org/eco/surveys/UK_Overview_ENG.pdf Figure 5.

But this simple insight raises another problem with austerity: the dreaded "r-g trap."

This formula $\Delta Debt\_1/GDP\_1=(r\text{-}g)*Debt\_0/GDP\_0+primedef$ is of great import in this debate. It shows that the change in the debt ratio (debt as a share of GDP) in the next period is a sum of the primary deficit (the deficit net of interest costs) and the previous debt ratio times the gap between the interest rate of sovereign debt (r) and the nominal GDP growth (g). If the nominal growth rate is higher than the average yield on government debt (so r-g is negative), this part of the equation reduces the next period's debt ratio, and visa versa.

In the US, r-g has been solidly negative in recent years. According to an important new data set of these variables developed by Kogan and Rejeski (forthcoming), from 2010-2013, the average for r was 2.2% while that of g was 3.6%. The US debt ratio grew in those years, of course, as a function of the last term in the equation: the budget deficit expanded as the great recession took hold. But it would have grown more quickly had r>g.

That inequality is currently making it very hard for various European embracers of austerity measures to get out from under their sovereign debt problems. For example, average nominal GDP growth in Spain averaged about -0.5%, 2010-12, while their 10-year bond yield rose from around four to five percent. Greece, Italy, and Portugal also remain stuck in the vise of this unforgiving arithmetic, contributing to increases in their debt ratios even as their deficits decline.

In sum, and with recognition that each countries' circumstances are unique—recall Corsetti's view that the austerity case was stronger in Italy than say, the UK—contractionary policy in demand constrained economies has proven to be damaging to growth and unemployment. In some cases, particularly those exposed to both high yields on sovereign debt and slow nominal growth rates, austerity appears to be self-defeating, whacking both growth and debt reduction.

Growth and Fiscal Consolidation

Even deficit doves (like myself) would voice concern if government expenditures consistently outpaced receipts such that public deficits and debt rose throughout good times and bad. I'll say more about this below, including the economic rationale for the SH ("structural hawk") part of the acronym in the title. But in this section, I examine, using the US case, the ebbs and flows of deficits and debt as a share of GDP, looking for patterns that suggest more economically suitable guidance than austerity.

We begin with Figure 4, showing a medium term time series of revenues, outlays, and publically held debt, all as shares of GDP from 1973-2012.[5] Focusing first on revenues and outlays, at least up until recently, they do not fluctuate all that much, nor do they tell an obvious story of a history profligate fiscal policy wherein policy makers refused to make "hard choices" while building up unsustainable burdens for "our grandchildren."

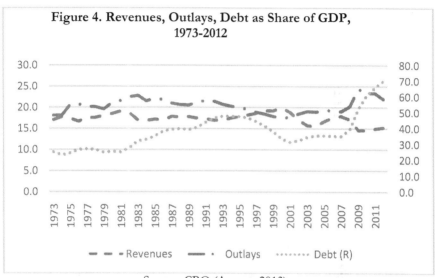

Figure 4. Revenues, Outlays, Debt as Share of GDP, 1973-2012

Source: CBO (August, 2013).

Spending has exceeded outlays for most of these years—the average deficit as a share of GDP, 1973-2007 was -2.4%--though prior to the Great Recession, the debt ratio increased only in the 1980s, as the Reagan deficits, caused in part by higher than average spending and lower than average revenues, exceeded "primary balance." I speak to the legendary Clinton surplus years below, but here we see the opposite of the Reagan pattern: higher revenues and lower spending, leading to primary balance in the latter 90s and surpluses, 1998-2001.

The deficits of the George W. Bush years appear to be less of function of runaway spending (a frequent conservative critique of those years) and more that of diminished revenues, i.e., the tax cuts of 2001 and 2003 (more on this below). Though part of the decline was due to the 2001 recession, revenues fell to 15.6% of GDP in 2004, the lowest in the figure prior to the recent recession. This reversed the decline in the debt ratio, though even with the

---

[5] CBO data. One reason for not going back further in time is that these are the only data available as of writing that incorporate the extensive GDP revisions that occurred in the summer of 2013. In the next figure, I ignore this data limitation, though the basic story the series tell is decidedly unchanged.

lower tax regime, the G.W. Bush deficits significantly diminished and were only 1.1% in 2007, leading to a brief period of debt stabilization before the recession.

This brief and cursory history is actually revealing. First, though fluctuations due both to the fiscal policy and the business cycles are evident, outside of recessions, receipts and outlays never drifted very far from each other. As noted, even after the Bush tax cuts reduced federal taxation to historically low levels, the debt ratio stabilized as the deficit fell toward the end of the 2000s business cycle. It is hard to square these trends with an American debate over our supposed profligate fiscal policy, a debate that has fed strongly into the austerity craze.

Second, the role of growth is a critical piece of the dynamics in the figure 4. The Clinton surpluses are typically hailed as a triumph of responsible fiscal policy, and, in fact, the first Clinton budget set the stage for the higher revenues and lower spending that can be seen quite clearly as leading to the surpluses in the figure 4. But what were the relative roles of policy and growth in those years?

In fact, Clinton-year fiscal policies explain at most a third of the swing to surplus, and even less depending on where we start counting during his presidency. Since the Congressional Budget Office (CBO) projects deficits numerous years into the future, we can look at the actual impact of Clinton-year fiscal policies compared to what the CBO thought would occur. Before the first Clinton budget took effect, the budget agency was expecting deficits of around 4% of GDP per year throughout the 1990s. But, as noted, the deficit was more than erased by 1998.

How much of that swing was due to policy changes? Looking over the full period that Clinton's fiscal policies were in place, basically 1993-2001, policy explains one-third of the swing. Looking over a shorter sub-period, starting in 1996, policy explains none of the swing. That is, in 1996, with the policy-generated revenue increases and spending cuts already in the CBO baseline, the budget agency still predicted a deficit of 2.7% of GDP in 2000. Moreover, actual fiscal policy changes post-96 added slightly to the deficit. Yet, by 2000, the budget surplus was 2.4% of GDP.[6]

In other words, while fiscal policy of course matters, given spending and receipts within historical ranges, the variable that matters most is growth.

Surely, fiscal hawks would argue that there were "endogenous" growth dynamics in play here, as financial markets rewarded fiscal rectitude with low interest rates, which in turn boosted growth. There may be something to this, though the fact was that interest rates weren't particularly low in those years. In fact, both corporate bond and 10-year Treasuries were lower in the G.W.

---

[6] These points are featured in the forthcoming book "Getting Back to Full Employment," by the author and Dean Baker.

Bush years than in the latter 1990s. Though deficit hawks often make this crowding out argument—government borrowing crowds out private borrowing, leading to higher interest rates—the evidentiary record is weak, particularly in periods of economic slack. In this regard, it is notable that since 1979, the actual unemployment rate has been higher than the non-accelerating inflation rate of unemployment (NAIRU), as estimated by CBO, two-thirds of the time; before that, labor markets were slack by this measure one-third of the time.[7]

This type of thinking about the fiscal challenge in a weak economy pushes one towards focusing on output gaps rather than fiscal gaps. Figure 5 plots the real GDP output gap against the change in the debt-to-GDP ratio. The output gap is simply the percent difference between actual and potential GDP. For example, a value of 5% on this metric means that real economic output is above capacity, at least according to CBO's measure of potential GDP. The other variable in figure 5 is simply the percentage point change in the debt ratio.

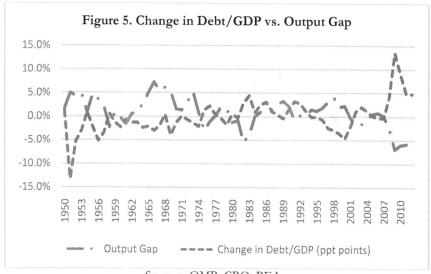

Figure 5. Change in Debt/GDP vs. Output Gap

Sources: OMB, CBO, BEA.

The negative correlation is strong—the correlation coefficient is -.77—and certain time periods bear closer scrutiny. Contrast, for example, the 1980s with the 1990s. In the former decade, output gaps were largely negative and the debt ratio increased for most of the decade. The 1990s, on

---

[7] The CBO estimates a quarterly NAIRU from 1949-the present (and beyond by forecast). I made this calculation by comparing the actual jobless rate with their NAIRU and taking the share of quarters in each time period that the actual rate was above the NAIRU.

the other hand, provides a particularly clean view of this dynamic: as output gaps went from negative to positive, the debt ratio fell sharply. The most recent period covering the Great Recession and its aftermath provides a clear case of a large output gap leading to sharp growth in public debt.[8]

Of course, correlation does not prove causation, and economist Ken Rogoff, most notably, has controversially argued that at a certain level, debt rations become a drag on growth. However, his research in this area has been shown to be quite flawed, and recent analysis by Dube and others shows causality generally proceeding from growth to debt.

The evidence from the two prior sections thus argues that, aside from individual circumstances that prevail in specific economies, policy makers in demand constrained economies should focus on closing output gaps, not budget gaps. Yet in recent years they have typically not done so. Examining why that has been the case is the focus of the rest of this chapter.

How Did Fiscal Policy Get Turned Upside Down?

I identify three reasons why fiscal policy became so backwards in recent years. First, a strategy by Democrats to block the G.W. Bush tax cuts morphed from strategy to ideology. Second, a misunderstanding of the Clinton surpluses in ways alluded to above. And third, the use of deficit fear-mongering to achieve the goal of significantly shrinking the government sector.

During the early years of the G.W. Bush administration, the President proposed and Congress passed two tax-cut packages that quite sharply lowered the revenues flowing to the Treasury. During those debates, opponents of the cuts raised their negative impact on deficits and debt as a major concern. Such concerns proved to be justified. As Ruffing and Friedman show (2013), instead of slowly rising (see Figure 4 above), the debt ratio would have been falling in the latter 2000s but for the Bush tax cuts (war spending played a much smaller role).[9] In my terminology, G.W. Bush fiscal policy was that of an SD (structural dove), adding to the debt ratio throughout the expansion of the 2000s.

Many who were making those anti-tax-cut arguments cited the Clinton years as an instructive counter-example. The lesson of those years, they argued, was that by increasing taxes and restraining spending, the Clinton budgets both led to surpluses and assuaged bond markets leading to lowering borrowing costs, more investment, and faster growth. In fact, while fiscal policy in Clinton's first budget did lower projected deficits, as discussed

---

[8] Arin Dube, https://dl.dropboxusercontent.com/u/15038936/RR%20Timepath/ Dube_Growth_Debt_Causation.pdf. Also, Bivens and Irons, http://www.epi.org/publication/bp271/.
[9] http://www.cbpp.org/cms/?fa=view&id=3849 (see Figure 2).

above, economic growth was far the larger factor (the fact that much of this growth was a function of a dot.com bubble is a separate issue).

Together, these lines of attack against the Bush tax cuts in tandem with the over-emphasis on Clinton fiscal policy as the factor that led to surpluses, raised the budget deficit to a new level in the national debate. Deficit hawkish pundits, editorial pages, and policy makers knew two things: Clinton raised taxes, cut spending, and balanced the budget; Bush cut taxes, failed to restrain spending, and added to the debt ratio.

Again, reality was more complex. Economic growth was the major factor behind the Clinton surpluses, and while G.W. Bush's tax cuts clearly added to the deficit and debt, even under his highly imbalanced fiscal policy, the deficit-to-GDP ratio fell to about 1% in 2007. To be clear, this is no endorsement of his structural dovishness. The year 2007 was the last year of that business cycle expansion, and as I'll argue below, it's important to get the debt ratio on a downward path much sooner than that. But the collision of these two different approaches to fiscal policy in two back-to-back decades helped to construct a conventional wisdom about budget deficits as a national scourge that had more to do with cursory observation than economic analysis.

Another important factor in the evolution of these wrong-headed ideas was the partisan ideology that government should be much smaller as a share of the economy. For conservatives who shared this vision, elevating the issue of the budget deficit as a major national problem was and remains a highly effective strategy. If they could convince the public and their representatives that deficits had to be reduced no matter what, then cutting the federal budget should be a short step away.

Of course, at least in terms of arithmetic, it is not at all obvious that balancing budgets requires spending cuts; that could also be achieved by raising taxes. So, part of the conservative strategy has been to take higher tax revenues off the table. Similarly, some—though not all—in the conservative caucus aim to protect defense spending. That leaves the non-defense discretionary budget and the mandatory entitlement programs, and these are in fact the targets of conservatives who continue to cite the threat of budget deficits—even as they fall sharply.

An illuminating set of documents showing these dynamics in action are the recent budgets by House Republicans. These budgets have proposed to cut taxes sharply for those at the top of the income scale, slash food support and Medicaid, turn Medicare into a voucher program, and cut non-defense discretionary spending to historically unforeseen low levels.

This analysis of the House 2010 budget, from budget expert Robert Greenstein, provides some extensive detail of this goal of shrinking government (Greenstein is referring to CBO analysis of the House budget authored by Rep. Paul Ryan, a noted deficit hawk).[10]

"The CBO report, prepared at Chairman Ryan's request, shows that Ryan's budget path would shrink federal expenditures for everything other than Social Security, Medicare, Medicaid, the Children's Health Insurance Program (CHIP), and interest payments to just 3¾ percent of the gross domestic product (GDP) by 2050. Since, as CBO notes, "spending for defense alone has not been lower than 3 percent of GDP in any year [since World War II]" and Ryan seeks a high level of defense spending — he increases defense funding by $228 billion over the next ten years above the pre-sequestration baseline — the rest of government would largely have to disappear. That includes everything from veterans' programs to medical and scientific research, highways, education, nearly all programs for low-income families and individuals other than Medicaid, national parks, border patrols, protection of food safety and the water supply, law enforcement, and the like. (In the same vein, CBO also notes that spending for everything other than Social Security, Medicare, Medicaid, and interest "has exceeded 8 percent of GDP in every year since World War II."

Another interesting example comes from a recent policy suggestion by conservative economists Glenn Hubbard and Tim Kane.[11] They begin by citing an Admiral from the Joint Chiefs of Staff claiming that the national debt is the "single biggest threat to our national security." They then call for an amendment to the US Constitution that they call a balanced budget amendment but is really a spending cap: "Congress shall spend no more in the current year than it collected, on average, over the previous seven years."

Though they explicitly note that Congress can override the amendment in "national emergencies," such a rule seems clearly motivated by the desire to reduce the size of government and preclude Keynesian measures in downturn.

In sum, the over-interpretation of fiscal rectitude in the Clinton years (and conversely, the under-appreciation of the role of growth), the "structural dovishness" of the G.W. Bush years, and the ideological drive to shrink the size of government have contributed to our current predicament, where despite evidence to the contrary, austerity measures dominate fiscal policy.

---

[10] http://www.cbpp.org/cms/?fa=view&id=3708
[11] http://www.nytimes.com/2013/08/12/opinion/republicans-and-democrats-both-miscalculated.html

What Would a Better Fiscal Policy Look Like?

A fiscal policy for our time would be one where the budget deficit would temporarily expand as much as necessary to meet the shortfall in private demand, and then, when that demand was solidly driving the expansion, the deficit would move toward primary balance, followed by a decline in the debt-to-GDP ratio. Beyond that simple formulation, the magnitudes of Keynesian expansions of deficits in downturns and consolidation in recoveries is, of course, situational. To delve into the question of how large a stimulus package needs to be relative to the output gap is beyond the scope I've set out in this analysis, which is simply to point out that the first fiscal question in a downturn in advanced economies is not, "how can we most quickly get back to a balanced budget?" It's: "given what we know about the magnitude of fiscal multipliers is our budget deficit temporarily large enough to offset the demand contraction?"[12]

Granted, policy makers need to watch "all the dials," including rates of inflation and interest, in order to gauge the impact of fiscal policy on other key macro-variables. Cases where a rising debt ratio blows out rate spreads obviously require different fiscal policy stances to countries where bond yields of public debt remain low, even as deficits expand. However, economic theory predicts and evidence generally supports the latter, not the former.[13]

Some deficit doves will ask: why does the debt ratio need to come down in expansions? There are at least two good reasons for that. First, a higher stock of debt makes the government sector that much more vulnerable to interest rate spikes. With today's GDP closing in on $17 trillion in the US, compare debt ratios of 65% and 75%. That another $1.7 trillion against which higher interest rates must be assessed. That's no reason to avoid necessary increases in the debt ratio, but it is a good reason to lower the stock of public debt as a bona-fide recovery takes hold.

Second, a political economy rationale is that policy makers simply will be more reluctant to allow the debt ratio to rise in the next recession if it hasn't receded much from the last one. In this sense, a lower debt ratio at the end

---

[12] In this regard, the simplest place to start to answer this question is og/km, where og=real GDP output gap and km=the average Keynesian multiplier across the various methods of stimulus under consideration.

[13] I'm referring here to simple IS-LM theory and evidence in the case where interest rates are up against the zero-lower-bound. Here, since the LM curve is virtually horizontal (liquidity trap), theory predicts that deficit spending will increase demand without raising the interest rate.

of an expansion provides a better perch from which to offset the next downturn.[14]

And thus we arrive at the simple, though hopefully not too reductionist, adage that I hope will serve as a simple guideline for policy makers: CDSH, or cyclical dove, structural hawk. Purveyors of austerity are CH's—cyclical hawks—and evidence presented above suggests their approach is self-defeating. SD's—structural doves—contribute to another problem: by building up the debt ratio in good times, they leave the Treasury vulnerable to interest rate spikes and make it less likely that policy makers will engage in needed temporary stimulus in the next downturn. Also, they provide the ideologically driven budget cutters with an excellent prop to inveigh against.

CDSH's, on the other hand, allow the deficit to expand to offset temporary contractions, and then make sure that when a solid expansion is underway, the combination of a shrinking output gap, along with adequate revenues to meet desired spending, ensure that the budget moves to primary balance and below, in order to begin to reduce the debt ratio. It is notable that a key ingredient in this mix is strong economic growth. History is quite clear on this point: absent growth, the fiscal lift is much harder, another reason why austerity measures in demand constrained economies are self-defeating. It is not a coincidence that the only period of sustained reduction in the debt-to-GDP ratio over the past 30 years was the period of full employment in the 1990s.

---

[14] Kogan and Van de Water point out that it would take deficit savings of $900 billion over the next decade to stabilize the debt ratio at 72%, down from 76% in 2014. Outside of the 10-year window, the debt ratio would begin to climb again due largely to pressures from public health care costs. http://www.cbpp.org/files/7-10-13bud.pdf

8. Short- and Long-Run Alternatives to Austerity in the US

Robert Pollin, *Department of Economics and Political Economy Research Institute (PERI), University of Massachusetts-Amherst, pollin@econs.umass.edu.*

An alternative to austerity

Coming up with alternatives to the austerity agenda in the US begins with asking a different set of questions than those posed by the austerity hawks. Instead of asking how to bring down the US fiscal deficit to control the economy's supposed fiscal crisis, the question we should rather ask is: how do we eliminate mass unemployment and move the US economy onto a path of sustainable full employment?

There is a wide range of issues to address if we want to advance full employment as a serious alternative to today's dominant austerity agenda. These include issues around globalization, financialization and financial regulation, the inflation-unemployment trade-off, industrial policy, new progressive sources of tax revenues, and controlling health care costs. For the current discussion, I focus on only two issues that I consider central to the broader discussion. These are: 1) Creating an effective overall stimulus program in the short-run and 2) Permanently expanding decent employment opportunities in the long run through investments in the green economy and education.[1]

Short-run stimulus policies

Fiscal stimulus

The federal government is not in a fiscal crisis. As of mid-2013, interest payments on the federal debt were at a near-historic low of 5.9 percent of total government spending, a figure that is less than half the average under Ronald Reagan and George H.W. Bush. Especially with interest rates for the US government remaining at historically low levels, the federal government can and should expand spending on education, health care, public safety, family support, traditional infrastructure, the green economy, and unemployment insurance. Much of this funding can be used simply to stop

---

[1] I discuss these proposals and related ideas in greater depth in, among other places, Pollin (2012A, 2012B, and 2013).

and reverse the cuts we have seen in state and local government budgets. Overall, the amounts devoted to spending in these areas should be at least as large as the roughly $400 billion per year that was budgeted through the 2009 Obama stimulus program, the American Recovery and Reinvestment Act.

Fiscal policies such as I describe above have been widely discussed in progressive circles, including the Congressional Progressive Caucus (2013). I therefore focus on what I consider to be the equally important area of money and credit policies, where there has been much less attention paid to the possibilities for building viable alternatives to austerity.

Commercial banks' cash hoards

All such discussions should begin with the fact that US commercial banks are sitting on massive, historically unprecedented cash hoards. As of the most recent data from the first quarter of 2013, the commercial banks were carrying an unprecedented $1.8 trillion in cash reserves. This is equal to more than 11 percent of US GDP. The banks obtained most of this money because, from the end of 2008 through this writing in August 2013, the Federal Reserve has maintained the interest rate at which banks can borrow at nearly zero percent—that is, the banks have access to nearly unlimited liquid funds at no borrowing costs. The other big source of the banks' funds was the Fed's "quantitative easing" program, whereby the Fed purchased longer-term Treasury holdings from the banks.

Of course, banks need to maintain a reasonable supply of cash reserves as a safety cushion against future economic downturns. One of the main causes of the 2008-09 crisis and other recent financial crises was that banks' cash reserves were far too low. But increasing reserves to $1.8 trillion is certainly a new form of financial market excess.   It is true that a significant fraction of these funds need to be held by the banks to carry an adequate margin of safety in the currently highly risky environment. However, as I have analyzed elsewhere (Pollin 2012B), after making highly conservative assumptions about the safety requirements of the banks in the current environment, I concluded that a reserve fund of $600 billion for the commercial banks would provide a safety margin far beyond any previous historical experience as well as beyond current needs.   This means that about $1.2 trillion should be available to move into the economy as productive loans.

Escaping the liquidity trap

Of course, saying the money is available in abundance doesn't mean it is going to get channeled into job-generating investments. Private businesses operate to earn a profit. As such, the fact that banks are sitting on approximately $1.2 trillion in excess cash rather than lending these funds for productive purposes must mean that, at some level, they do not see adequate profit opportunities in the US economy today through investments and job creation.

Relative to previous recessions in the US and elsewhere, including the 1930s Depression itself, the conditions in credit markets over the Great Recession and subsequently are hardly unique. Indeed, this contemporary experience represents just the most recent variation on the classic problems in recessions in reaching a "liquidity trap" and trying to "push on a string." This is when banks would rather sit on cash hoards than risk making bad loans and businesses are not willing to accept the risk of new investments, no matter how cheaply they can obtain credit. The liquidity trap that has prevailed since the 2008-09 recession has served as a major headwind, counteracting the effects of what, on paper, had been a strongly expansionary macro policy stance through the 2009 Obama stimulus program.

Clearly, if businesses don't see investment opportunities, one overarching problem in the economy is insufficient demand from consumers, businesses, and the government itself as a purchaser. In the face of inadequate market demand, a federal government austerity agenda—cutting back on government spending—would then just make the economy's demand problem worse, not better. So step one for ending the liquidity trap has to be reversing the fiscal austerity agenda and instead refocusing on a viable federal stimulus.

However, the economy has also been operating with severe credit constraints, with small businesses, in particular, having been locked out of credit markets. We therefore need to explore a range of policy approaches that can reduce the level of risk for borrowers and lenders, and/or raise the costs for banks to continue holding cash hoards. I focus here on two ideas: extending federal loan guarantees for small businesses and taxing the excess reserves of banks.

Combining one carrot and one stick

This approach is simple, combining the use of one big carrot and one big stick to creating millions of new jobs quickly. The carrot would be measures to substantially reduce the level of risk being faced by both borrowers and lenders. This can be done through the federal government's existing loan guarantee program. In terms of practical implementation of such a program, the federal government does already operate various loan guarantee programs on a major scale. Thus, for 2012, the total level of loans guaranteed by the federal government was about $780 billion. This equals about 2.8 percent of all outstanding debt held by US households and domestic non-financial businesses. By far, the largest category of loan guarantees was housing subsidies, with about $130 billion going to businesses. The federal government should pursue an agenda to roughly triple as rapidly as possible its overall loan guarantee program to non-housing related businesses to about $450 billion in total, with the focus of the expansion on small businesses. That would entail an increase of guaranteed loans for small business of about $300 billion. This would represent a major expansion of the existing federal guarantee programs, while still remaining within the scale of existing overall programs. It would also be a huge benefit to small businesses, which—as the Republicans always emphasize—do indeed create significantly more jobs per dollar of spending than big businesses.

The stick would be for the federal government to tax the excess reserves now held by banks. This should create a strong disincentive for banks to continue holding massive cash hoards. It is difficult to know in advance what the appropriate tax rate should be for this purpose—probably in the range of 1-2 percent, but any such initiative should also allow Congress to operate with flexibility to adjust the rate as needed for channeling excess reserves into job-generating investments. For starters, the Fed needs to stop paying interest on bank reserves. It currently pays 0.25 percent on these accounts. Indeed, this whole initiative could be conducted through the Fed, as opposed to having Congress pass an excess reserve tax. The way they could do this is to establish a maximum level of reserves that they would allow banks to hold without facing a penalty for holding excess cash hoards.

One crucial feature of this combination of policies is that its impact on the federal budget will be negligible. Loan guarantees are contingent liabilities for the federal government. This means that, beyond some relatively modest increase in administrative costs, the government would incur costs from the loan guarantee program only as a result of defaults on the guaranteed loans. Even if we assumed, implausibly, that the default rate on the new loans was triple the proportion that prevailed in 2007, prior to the recession, this would still only increase the federal budget by less than one percent. Moreover, a significant share of this budgetary expense could be covered by the revenues generated by the excess reserve tax.

Austerity hawks should therefore take note: the carrot of a new loan guarantee program for small businesses and the stick of taxing the massive cash hoard now being held by commercial banks—with money they obtained nearly for free from the Fed's zero interest rate policy—would be a nearly cost-free approach to providing serious support for small businesses especially. This would enable small businesses to expand operations and begin to making the job-generating investments we need.

Clean energy and education investments for long-run prosperity

We can envision the path to creating a sustainable full-employment economy through considering some basic data on the job-creating effects of investing in clean energy and education relative to spending on fossil fuel energy and the military. Figure 1 below shows the level of job creation in each of four sectors—clean energy, education, fossil fuels and the military—for every $1 million in spending in these sectors. By a significant margin, education is the most effective source of job creation among these alternatives—about 27 jobs per $1 million in spending. Clean energy investments are second, with about 17 jobs per $1 million of spending. The US military creates about 11 jobs, while spending within the fossil fuel sector, by far the weakest source of job creation per dollars, creates about 5 jobs per $1 million.

Figure 1. Job Creation in the US through $1 Million in Spending, 2011

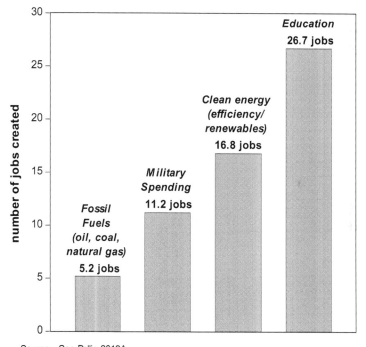

Source: See Pollin 2012A

Two main factors account for the differences in total job creation across sectors. The first is relative labor intensity, the amount of people as opposed to everything else a business utilizes in its operations. For example, a clean energy investment program utilizes far more of its budget to hire people than to acquire machines, supplies, land (either on- or offshore), or energy itself.

The second factor is relative domestic content per overall spending amount—how much of the work is done within the US rather than other countries. The clean energy sector relies much more than the fossil fuel sector on economic activities taking place within the United States—such as retrofitting homes or upgrading the electrical grid system—and less on imports.

Consider an agenda in which we transfer about 25 percent of total spending in both the military ($700 billion) and fossil fuel ($625 billion) sectors—that is, about $330 billion per year—in equal shares into education and clean energy? Before assessing the effect of this transfer of spending priorities on employment, we should of course also recognize their crucial and complimentary political and environmental benefits. Reducing the Pentagon's budget by 25 percent would simply return the military to its spending level prior to the wars in Iraq and Afghanistan to about 3 percent of US GDP. Cutting spending from fossil fuels and transferring it into clean energy, of course, reflects the imperative of controlling CO_2 emissions to fight global climate change. Finally, transferring approximately $165 billion per year into spending on education would represent a roughly 16 percent increase over the current total public spending level of about $1 trillion.

In terms of employment effects, the impact of a $330 billion annual spending shift out of the military and fossil fuel sectors and into education and clean energy would be dramatic. It would create about 4.8 million more jobs for a given level of total spending. The job expansion would be across all sectors and activities—i.e. new opportunities for highly paid engineers, researchers, lawyers and business consultants as well as for elementary school teachers, carpenters, bus drivers, cleaning staff at hotels, and lunch-counter workers at wind energy construction sites. Note also, that I am not proposing net increases in aggregate spending at all, but rather shifts in relative levels of spending between sectors that will generate a rise in overall labor intensity and domestic content for a given amount of spending.

In the context of today's economy, the injection of 4.8 million new jobs would reduce the unemployment rate by about one-third, from about 8 to 5 percent. Realistically, however, this kind of large-scale shift in spending economy-wide will not occur rapidly enough to affect today's unemployment rate in contrast with the short-term fiscal and credit policy measures discussed above. All the same, this large-scale shift in the country's investment priorities is capable of transforming the employment picture over the long-term. For example, assume that the unemployment rate were to fall over the next two years, if only to, say, 6.5 percent, through some combination of government interventions from the Obama administration and Federal Reserve along with something akin to a normal pattern of recovery. Within such a scenario, 4.8 million additional jobs through a spending shift that raises the labor intensity and domestic content of overall spending would drop the 6.5 unemployment rate to 3.4 percent. At this point, we would be at an unemployment rate where, during both the 1960s and 1990s, average wages rose significantly because worker bargaining power increased. In short, this kind of shift in investment priorities—toward clean energy and education and away from fossil fuels and the military—can be the foundation for building a sustainable full employment economy.

The proposals I have sketched here show that is not difficult to develop viable alternatives to this austerity agenda. The real challenge with all such alternatives is whether progressives can develop the political strength to force these ideas onto the mainstream policy agenda as effective tools for reversing the ongoing descent into austerity.

References

Congressional Progressive Caucus (2013), Back to Work Budget, Washington, DC: http://cpc.grijalva.house.gov/back-to-work-budget/

Pollin, Robert (2012A), *Back to Full Employment*, Cambridge, MA: MIT Press.

Pollin, Robert (2012B), "The Great US Liquidity Trap of 2009 – 11: Are We Stuck Pushing on Strings? *Review of Keynesian Economics*, 1:1, pp. 55-76.

Pollin, Robert (2013), "Austerity Economics and the Struggle for the Soul of US Capitalism," *Social Research*, 80:3, Fall, forthcoming.

III
Making Finance Serve The Real Economy

9. Making Finance Serve the Real Economy

Thomas I. Palley, Senior Economic Policy Adviser, AFL-CIO, *mail@thomaspalley.com*

Rethinking the role of finance

In the wake of the financial crisis of 2008, financial sector reform has been a major policy focus. However, that focus has been almost exclusively on the issue of "stability" and preventing a repeat of the crisis, and there has been little debate about the broader role of finance in shaping economic developments over the past thirty years.

This silence on the broader role of finance serves a political purpose. By restricting the reform debate to the narrow issue of stability, the economic winners have been able to shut down the case for deeper economic reform.

Financial markets have a broader social purpose than just the efficient allocation of capital on behalf of shareholders. That broader purpose is to contribute to the delivery of "shared prosperity", which can be defined as full employment with rising incomes and contained income inequality. Today, we clearly don't have shared prosperity, and a big reason for that is the economic and political power of finance.

Finance and the destruction of shared prosperity

To understand how finance has undermined shared prosperity requires a little history. Pre-1980 the US economy could be described as a Keynesian wage-led growth model, as illustrated in Figure 1. The economic logic of the model was as follows. Productivity growth drove wage growth which fuelled demand. That drove full employment which provided the incentive to invest, which drove productivity growth.

Within this economic model, finance was characterized as a form of public utility governed by New Deal regulation. The role of finance was to (1) provide business and entrepreneurs with finance for investment; (2) provide households with mortgage finance for home acquisition; (3) provide business and households with insurance services; (4) provide households with saving instruments to meet future needs; and (5) provide business and households with transactions services.

Figure 1. The 1945-75 virtuous circle of Keynesian growth model

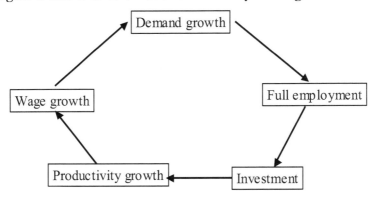

Figure 2. Productivity and real average hourly wage and compensation of US non-supervisory workers, 1947-2009

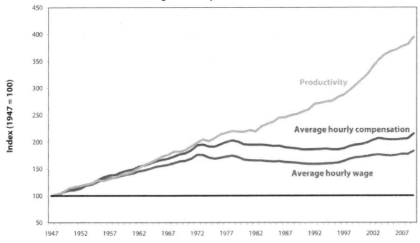

Source: EPI analysis of Bureau of Economic Analysis and
Bureau of Labor Statistics Data

After 1980, the Keynesian wage-led growth model and public utility model of finance was gradually pulled apart and dismantled. A first critical change was the implementation of economic policies that helped sever the link between wages and productivity growth. A second critical change was the dismantling of the New Deal system of financial regulation via deregulation, combined with refusal to regulate new financial developments and innovations. The impact of the dismantling of the wage – productivity growth link is captured in Figure 2 which shows how average hourly wages and compensation stagnated after 1980 despite continuing productivity growth.

As illustrated in Figure 3, the new model can be described as a neoliberal policy box that fences workers in and pressures them from all sides. On the left hand side, the corporate model of globalization put workers in international competition via global production networks that are supported by free trade agreements and capital mobility. On the right hand side, the "small" government agenda attacked the legitimacy of government and pushed persistently for deregulation regardless of dangers. From below, the labor market flexibility agenda attacked unions and labor market supports such as the minimum wage, unemployment benefits, employment protections, and employee rights. From above, policymakers abandoned the commitment of full employment, a development that was reflected in the rise of inflation targeting and the move toward independent central banks controlled by financial interests. The result was a new system characterized by wage stagnation and income inequality in which the problem of demand shortage was papered over by debt-financed consumption and asset price inflation.

Figure 3. The neoliberal policy box

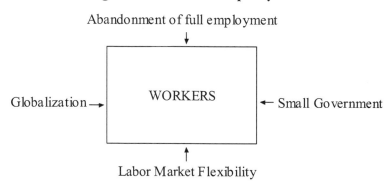

Finance played a critical role in both creating and maintaining the new economic model, the hallmarks of which are wage stagnation and increased income inequality; increased importance of the financial sector relative to the real sector; and transfer of income from the real sector to the financial sector. Table 1 shows how the financial sector increased as a share of GDP and how financial sector profits increased as a share of non-financial sector profits.

Table 1. Selected indicators of the growth of the financial sector relative to the overall economy.

	FIRE output/ GDP (%)	Financial/ Non-financial profits (%)	Household debt/ GDP (%)
1973	13.6	20.1	45.3
1979	14.4	19.7	49.9
1989	17.9	26.2	60.5
2000	20.1	39.3	70.3
2007	20.4	44.6	98.2

Note: FIRE= finance, insurance, and real estate.
Source: Palley (2013a), Tables 2.6, 2.7, and 2.11

The process whereby financial sector interests came to dominate the economy is now widely referred to as "financialization". Figure 4 shows the three main conduits of financialialization. First, finance used its political power to promote the economic policies on which the new model rests. Thus, finance lobbied for financial deregulation; supported the shift of macroeconomic policy away from focusing on full employment to focusing on inflation; supported corporate globalization and expanding international capital mobility; supported privatization, the regressive tax agenda, and the shrinking of the state; and supported the attack on unions and workers.

Figure 4. Main conduits of financialization

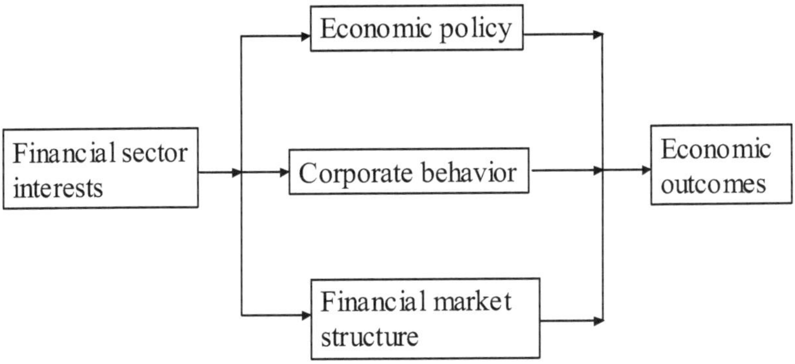

Second, finance took control of American business and forced it to adopt financial sector behaviors and perspectives. This change was accomplished via increased actual and threatened use of hostile takeovers, hedge fund activism, and increased use of massive stock option awards for top management that aligned management's interest with that of Wall Street. The resulting change in business behavior was justified using the rationale of shareholder value maximization. The result was a widespread use of leveraged buyouts that burdened firms with unprecedented levels of debt; the adoption of a short-term business perspective and impossibly high required rates of return that undercut long-term real investment; growing reliance on off-shoring and abandonment of a business commitment to community and country; and adoption of exceedingly generous Wall Street-styled pay packages for top management and boards of directors.

Third, the deregulated financial system provided the credit that financed borrowing and asset price bubbles that filled the "demand shortage" created by wage stagnation and increased inequality. As shown in Table 1, household debt rose as a share of GDP from 45.3% in 1973 to 98.2% in 2007, just prior to the financial crisis.

Viewed in this light, financialization is at the very core of current economic difficulties. Finance drove the policies that undermined shared prosperity, and then fuelled a thirty year credit bubble that papered over the demand shortage caused by worsening income distribution. That created an unstable financial system which collapsed when the credit bubble burst.

Now, after the financial crisis, the US economy is stuck in stagnation because of deteriorated income distribution and the massive structural trade deficit that, together, undercut domestic demand needed for full employment.

Putting finance back in the box

Restoring shared prosperity will require rebuilding the wage-productivity growth link and restoring full employment, and this will have to be done within the additional new constraints imposed by the requirement of environmental sustainability. That is a massive task requiring a range of different policies regarding labor markets, the international economy, the public sector, the environment, and macroeconomic policy. Given the critical role of finance, it also requires regaining control over finance so that it again serves the real economy, rather than the real economy serving finance.

One part of the challenge is political and concerns campaign finance reform. The political power of finance rests on money, which is why it is so critical to reduce the role of money in politics. Absent political reform, finance will be able to distort the democratic process and block necessary economic policy reform.

A second part of the challenge is changing corporate behavior. That requires corporate governance reform that makes business more accountable, changes incentives that promote current business practice, and recognizes the interests of stakeholders other than shareholders.

A third challenge is to regain control over financial markets. Figure 5 illustrates a four part program that puts financial markets back in the box so that they promote shared prosperity rather than destructive speculation and inequality. The top edge of the box concerns monetary policy where there is need to restore a commitment to full employment; to abandon a rigid ultra-low inflation target; and to recognize that monetary policy can permanently influence the level of economic activity.[1]

Figure 5. Putting finance back in the box

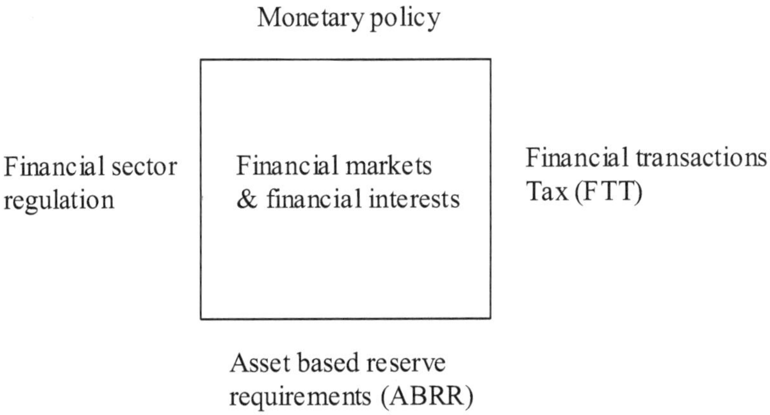

Monetary policy

Financial sector regulation

Financial markets & financial interests

Financial transactions Tax (FTT)

Asset based reserve requirements (ABRR)

The left edge of the box concerns the need for tough regulations that impose appropriate capital and liquidity requirements on financial institutions, and also bar banks from engaging in speculative activity using FDIC insured deposits - the so-called Volker rule (see Taub, chapter 13 in this volume). Of course, regulation must be also enforced which speaks to importance of a good government agenda that ensures the integrity and operational efficiency of regulatory agencies.

The right edge of the box concerns the need for a financial transactions tax (FTT). An FTT can raise revenue, help shrink the financial sector, and discourage damaging speculative transactions (see Palley, 2001; Baker, chapter 10 in this volume).

Lastly, the bottom edge of the box advocates the Federal Reserve institute a system of asset based reserve requirements (ABRR) that covers the entire financial sector, including shadow banks and hedge funds (Palley, 2003, 2009). ABRR extend margin requirements to a wide array of assets held by financial institutions. Financial firms have to hold reserves against different classes of assets, and the regulatory authority sets adjustable reserve requirements on the basis of its concerns with each asset class. By adjusting the reserve requirement on each asset class, the central bank can change the return on that asset class thereby affecting incentives to invest in the asset class.

---

[1] For a more detailed and extensive program of reform for monetary policy see Palley (2013b).

The US house price bubble showed central banks cannot manage the economy with just interest rate policy targeted on inflation and unemployment. Doing that leaves the economy exposed to financial excess. Interest rate policy must be therefore supplemented by quantitative balance sheet controls, which is the role of ABRR.

ABRR provide a new set of policy instruments that can target specific financial market excess by targeting specific asset classes, leaving interest rate policy free to manage the overall macroeconomic situation. ABRR can be adjusted on a targeted discretionary basis and thereby provide a powerful counter-cyclical balance sheet control, ABRR can also help prevent asset bubbles via increased requirements on over-heated asset categories. And they are particularly good for targeting house price bubbles since reserve requirement can be increased on new mortgages. Additionally, ABRR increase the demand for reserves by compelling banks to hold additional reserves, which can help the Federal Reserve exit the current period of quantitative easing and avoid future inflation.

Finally, ABRR can be used to promote socially desirable investments and "green" investments needed to address climate change. Loans for such investment projects can be given a negative reserve requirement that can be credited against other reserve requirements, thereby encouraging banks to finance those projects in order to earn the credit. In short, ABRR provide a comprehensive framework for collaring the financial sector and ensuring it promotes shared prosperity.

Conclusion: beyond orthodox economics

We live in an age of market worship. Orthodox economics fuels that worship and it also gives special standing to financial markets which are represented as the most perfect form of market. Of course, there is also some critique of the functional efficiency and casino aspects of financial markets, but those critiques stop far short of the financialization critique.[2] Consequently, orthodox diagnoses of the financial crisis and policy recommendations stop far short of what is needed to put finance back in the box.

The economic evidence clearly shows the need to make finance serve the real economy, rather than having the real economy serve finance as is now the

---

[2] Tobin (1984) noted that financial markets actually finance very little investment which, instead, is largely financed by retained profits. He also noted that many financial market activities may be unproductive so that bankers, brokers, and traders are paid far more than they contribute to economic production. Hirschleifer (1971) made an even earlier critique of financial markets in which he argued financial markets could lower real output to the extent that they were *de facto* casinos because operating the casino costs a lot. Most recently, Cechetti and Kharroubi (2012), from the Bank of International Settlements, have reported that too large a financial sector lowers growth.

case. It can be done. The challenge is to get a hearing for policies that will do so. Meeting that challenge requires getting new economic ideas on the table, which is why the debate about economics and the economy is so important. However, the road to policy change runs through politics. That means making finance serve the real economy also requires breaking the political power of finance, which is why campaign finance reform, electoral reform and popular political engagement are so important too.

References

Baker, D. (2013) "The need to rein in the financial sector", Chapter 11 in Palley and Horn (eds.), *Restoring Shared Prosperity: A Policy Agenda from Leading Keynesian Economists*, CreateSpace, forthcoming.

Cechetti, S.G. and Kharroubi, E. (2012) "Reassessing the impact of finance on growth," BIS Working Paper No. 381, Bank of International Settlements, Basel, Switzerland.

Hirshleifer, J. (1971) "The private and social value of information and the reward to inventive activity," *American Economics Review*, 61: 561-74.

Palley, T. I (2013a) *Financialization: The Macroeconomics of Finance Capital Domination*, Macmillan/Palgrave, 2013.

Palley, T.I. (2013b) "Monetary policy and central banking after the crisis: the implications of rethinking macroeconomic theory," in G. Epstein and M. Wolfson (eds.), *The Handbook on Political Economy of Financial Crises*, Oxford: Oxford University Press.

Palley, T.I. (2009) "A better way to regulate financial markets: asset based reserve requirements," Economists' Committee for Safer, Accountable, Fair and Efficient Financial Reform, University of Massachusetts, Amherst   available   at http://www.peri.umass.edu/fileadmin/pdf/other_publication_types/SA FERbriefs/SAFER_issue_brief15.pdf

Palley, T.I. (2003) "Asset price bubbles and the case for asset based reserve requirements," *Challenge*, 46 (May/June), 53 – 72.

Palley, T.I. (2001) "Destabilizing Speculation and the Case for an International Currency Transactions Tax," *Challenge*, 44 (May/June), 70 - 89.

Taub, J. (2013), "Delays, dilutions and delusions: Implementing the Dodd-Frank Act," Chapter 13 in T. Palley and G. Horn (eds.), *Restoring Shared Prosperity: A Policy Agenda from Leading Keynesian Economists*, CreateSpace, forthcoming.

Tobin, J. (1984), "On the efficiency of the financial system," *Lloyds Bank Review*, 153, 1 – 15.

10. The Need to Rein in the Financial Sector

Dean Baker, *Center for Economic and Policy Research, 1611 Connecticut Ave., NW, Washington, DC 20009, baker@cepr.net*

The harmful effects of a bloated financial sector

The financial sector has exploded in size in most wealthy countries over the last three decades. There are reasons for believing this expansion has worsened economic outcomes by a variety of measures. While the financial sector plays an essential role in allocating capital, a bloated financial sector can be a drag on the economy. This paper outlines the case for reducing the size of the financial sector and suggests a financial transactions tax as the best means for bringing about this result.

There are two main reasons for believing that the current size of the financial sector is harmful to the growth of the economy. First, the size itself suggests an enormous waste of resources. An efficient financial sector is a small financial sector. The second reason is that a bloated financial sector can lead to the sort of instability that has substantial effects on the real economy. Specifically, a bloated financial sector can lead to the sort of asset bubbles that we saw in most wealthy countries in the last decade, the collapse of which has led to the longest period of stagnation since the Great Depression.

On the first point, it is important to keep in mind that finance is an intermediate good, like trucking. It does not provide direct value to the economy like the food, housing, or health care sectors. If the financial sector expands relative to the size of the economy, without obviously performing its role more effectively, then it would be evidence of waste in the same way that a vast expansion of the trucking sector would be evidence of waste.

The financial sector as a whole has expanded over the last three decades, but the fastest growth has been in the narrow investment banking and commodities and securities trading sectors. In 1970, the narrowly defined financial sector (commodities and securities trading and investment banking) accounted for 0.5 percent of employee compensation in the private sector.[1] Its share had risen to 2.3 percent in 2010. This difference would be equal to

---

[1] Bureau of Economic Analysis, National Income and Products Accounts, Table 6.2B, Lines 55 plus 59, divided by line 1 and Table 6.2D, line 59 divided by line 1. (These data pre-date the 2013 revisions. Post-revision data are not available at this level of detail.) Compensation is used rather value-added because valued-added data are not available at this level of industry detail although the calculation in the text assumes that value added is proportional to labor compensation.

$250 billion annually given the size of the US economy in 2013. The growth of this sector implies an enormous diversion of resources from other sectors of the economy.

This sort of growth could be justified if it was associated with a financial sector that was more effectively carrying through its role, however it would be difficult to argue that this is the case. From the side of investment this should mean higher rates of productivity growth, as capital is allocated to better uses. At the most basic level this story hardly fits the main patterns of productivity growth in the Post-World War II era. Productivity growth averaged 2.8 percent in the years from 1947 to 1973. In the years since 1973 it has only averaged 1.8 percent. Even if we take the years since the productivity speed-up began in 1995, growth has only averaged 2.3 percent.[2]

It is always possible to maintain that productivity growth would have been worse without the expansion of the financial sector in recent decades, but there is little evidence to support this case. Cecchitti and Kharoubbi (2012) examined growth across countries and found an inverted U-shaped pattern between the size of the financial sector and growth. When the financial sector is very small relative to the size of the economy, a larger financial sector is associated with more rapid growth. However once the financial grows large, further expansion is associated with slower growth. Most wealthy countries, like the United States and the United Kingdom, have financial sectors of the size where further expansion would be a drag on growth, according this research.

The study also examined productivity growth by industry to try to determine the mechanisms through which an expanded financial sector slows growth. It found that the industries that saw the sharpest decline in the rate of productivity growth were either R&D intensive or alternatively heavily dependent on external financing. The first finding can be easily explained by the financial sector pulling away people with sophistical mathematical skills from other industries. This would mean that rather working in software, chemistry, or other sectors that might require strong math skills, workers with sophisticated math skills end up designing complex algorithms for profitable trading in countries with large financial sectors.

The other finding would be consistent with a view that financial speculation is actually raising the cost of capital for firms trying to expand. In other words, it would mean that the financial sector is pulling away so much capital from the economy for speculative purposes that it makes it more difficult to raise new capital.

The second main argument against an oversized financial sector is that it creates a political economy that is conducive to destabilizing bubbles. Since

---

[2] The superior performance of the early post-war decades is even more pronounced using a net measure of output (Baker, 2007).

the sample in this case is essentially just the early post-war period, when the wealthy countries did not have bloated financial sectors, and the more recent period in which they did have bloated financial sectors, the argument has to be largely descriptive.

In the earlier period there was an accord between manufacturing firms and workers in which productivity growth was largely passed on in the form of higher wages. In the three decades following World War II real wages rose at more than a 1.5 percent annual rate. This had the benefit for firms of sustaining high levels of demand, even if they might individually prefer to pay their workers less.

This accord broke down in the last three decades. There were many factors behind its collapse, but one point is clear, financial firms do not benefit in the same way from wage growth as manufacturing firms. In fact, insofar as they are invested in debt with fixed nominal interest rates, they will have a direct interest in acting to minimize inflation, even at the cost of high unemployment and slow wage growth. The growing political power of the financial sector has undoubtedly been a factor in the increased focus of central banks on inflation in this period.

However the failure of wages, and therefore consumption, to keep pace with productivity growth, means that the economy can often face sustained periods of below full employment levels of demand. This was the basis for the bubble driven growth that the United States has seen over the last two decades.[3]

In the 1990s the Clinton administration vigorously pursued a policy of deficit reduction, with tax increases and spending cuts. These measures, while effective in reducing the deficit, undermined an important source of demand for the economy. The Federal Reserve Board responded to the weakening of demand by lowering interest rates. The direct impact of lower interest rates on demand is generally limited as none of the components of demand are very sensitive to lower interest rates.

However, lower interest rates did help to fuel a stock market bubble. The stock market by most measures was already well above its long-term average price to earnings ratios by the early 1990s. The market continued to rise rapidly over the course of the decade, eventually peaking in 2000 at a price to earnings ratio that was more than twice its long-term average. This bubble was the fuel for the rapid growth that the economy saw in the second half of the 1990s.

Its main impact was on consumption as the creation of $10 trillion in bubble equity increased consumption through the wealth effect by $300-$400 billion a year. This pushed the savings rate to what were at the time record low levels. The stock bubble also led to somewhat of an investment boom as

---

[3] This argument is laid out in more depth in Baker, 2008.

it suddenly became possible for even ill-conceived Internet start-ups to raise hundreds of millions or even billions of dollars by issuing stock.

When the stock bubble burst, the economy again suffered from a serious lack of demand. While the 2001 recession is often viewed as short and mild, the economy did not pass its pre-recession level of employment until February of 2005. It was at the time the longest period without job creation since the Great Depression. In response to the weakness of the economy the Federal Reserve Board lowered the federal funds rate to 1.0 percent, the lowest rate since the early 1950s.

The economy did eventually recovery from the 2001 recession and start to create jobs again, but this time it was on the back of a housing bubble. House prices, which had historically just kept pace with the overall rate of inflation, hugely outpaced inflation in the decade from 1997 to 2007. Over this period, the rise in house prices exceeded the rate of inflation by more than 70 percentage points creating more than $8 trillion in bubble driven growth. This growth was driven on the one hand by near record levels of construction in the years 2002-2006 and by a consumption boom resulting from the housing wealth effect. At the peak of the housing bubble, the savings rate fell to levels even lower than at the peak of the stock bubble in 2000. The bursting of this bubble gave us the financial crisis and the Great Recession. More than five and a half years after the start of the recession the economy is still operating well below its potential by any measure.

While bubbles may not be an inevitable feature of the current economy, there clearly is more room for them in an economy that must rely on low interest rates to sustain demand, rather than wage growth. As long as finance plays a leading role in the US economy, it is likely that policymakers will be wrestling with containing bubbles or cleaning up the wreckage after the fact.

There is one other important point worth noting about finance. It is a leading generator of inequality in the economy. The pay of high-end earners in the industry is considerably higher than in other sectors of the economy. Philippon and Reshef (2009) show that wages in the financial industry rose much more rapidly than elsewhere in the economy in the 1980s and 1990s. By the peak of the bubble they were far out of line with wages in other industries. They conclude that most of the gap in wages was due to rents, not human capital.

The inequality that results from some of the exorbitant pay packages going to top executives and traders present another reason to be concerned about the financial sector. Many of the wealthiest people in the country have gained their fortunes in the financial industry. In some cases this may have been attributable to financial innovation or savvy investment strategies, however in many cases individuals and firms were gaining wealth by manipulating markets or engaging in financial engineering of little value to the economy.[4]

Downsizing the Financial Sector

Bringing the financial sector down to size and restoring it to its proper function of serving the real economy will not be a simple task. The sector has enormous political power and it is not shy about using this power to protect its revenue and profits. One policy that would go far towards downsizing the industry would be a financial transactions tax (FTT).

This is a policy that could raise enormous amounts of revenue for the government directly at the expense of the industry. We also know that it will not obstruct the functioning of financial markets, since plausible levels of the tax would only raise the cost of transactions back to levels that they were at two to three decades ago, when markets were already large and liquid.

There are already many countries that have FTTs in place, including the UK, Switzerland, China, and India. Based on the experience of these and other countries we know that an FTT can be enforced and raise substantial sums of money. The UK has raised between 0.2-0.3 percent of GDP from its tax over the last decade. This is impressive since the tax only applies to stock trades and allows for easy evasion through derivative contracts.

In the 1980s Japan raised an amount of revenue that exceeded one percent of GDP from its broadly based text. Pollin et.al (2003) calculated that a broadly based tax in the United States, scaled to UK tax of 0.5 percent on roundtrip stock trades, could raise more than 1.0 percent of GDP.

An FTT would also be desirable from a distributional standpoint since the overwhelming majority of the burden would be borne by the industry itself. Most studies find that the elasticity of trading with respect to costs is close to -1.0, which means that trading volume can be expected to decline roughly in proportion to the size of a tax (SOURCE). This implies that in response to an FTT, an average pension fund or individual with a retirement savings account will reduce their trading volume by enough so that the total amount they spend on trading (including the tax) is little changed. As a result, almost the whole burden of the tax would come out of the revenue and the profits of the industry.

This is exactly the result that those concerned about the excessive size and power of the financial industry should want to see. Trading that serves an economic purpose will be little affected by taxes on derivative trades of 0.01

---

[4] The New York Times documented how Goldman Sachs was able to earn billions of dollars through its control of the major aluminum warehouse in the United States ("A Shuffle of Aluminum, but to Banks It is Pure Gold, 7-20-13:A1
[http://www.nytimes.com/2013/07/21/business/a-shuffle-of-aluminum-but-to-banks-pure-gold.html?pagewanted=all]

percent or stock trades of 0.5 percent. (The rate being considered by the EU is just 0.1 percent on stock trades.) However, many short-term trades that are made for speculative purposes or to seize on market momentum are likely to be discouraged by a tax that will eat up much or all of their expected gains. This would lead to much less trading and a considerably smaller financial sector.

A financial transactions tax is certainly not the only change that is needed to reform the financial system, but it will go a long way to bringing it down to size and eliminating the basis for many of the rents in the sector. It would be difficult to envision a more useful way to raise revenue for the government.

References

Baker, Dean (2008), *Plunder and Blunder: The Rise and Fall of the Bubble Economy*, San Francisco: Polipoint Press.

Baker, D. (2007), "The Productivity to Paycheck Gap: What the Data Show," Washington, DC: Center for Economic and Policy Research.

Cechetti, S., annd Kharoubbi, E. (2012), "Reassessing the Impact of Finance on Growth," Bank of International Settlements, http://www.google.com/url?sa=t&rct=j&q=&esrc=s&source=web&cd =1&ved=0CC0QFjAA&url=http%3A%2F%2Fwww.bis.org%2Fpubl%2 Fwork381.pdf&ei=jkgNUuOzHoKRygHC1YAQ&usg=AFQjCNGhOF CdGDhtZaWQlRneiLEMr6E0ew&sig2=jWBXpfqgmAWsccgy5APwtQ &bvm=bv.50768961,d.aWc

Philippon, T. and Reshef, A. (2009), "Wages and Human Capital in the US Financial Industry: 1909-2006, National Bureau of Economic Research Working Paper, #14644

Pollin, R., Baker, D., and Schaberg, M. (2003), "Security Transactions Taxes for US Financial Markets," *Eastern Economic Review*, Vol. 29, No. 4 (Fall 2003): 527-558, http://www.peri.umass.edu/236/hash/aef97d8d65/ publication/172/

11. Restructuring Finance to Better Serve Society

Gerald Epstein[1], Professor of Economics and Co-Director, Political Economy Research Institute (PERI), University of Massachusetts, Amherst, gepstein@econs.umass.edu.

Introduction

The Great Financial Crisis of 2008, from which we have yet to recover, has called into question the contributions of modern financial institutions and practices to social well-being. Such concerns have been raised even by those in surprisingly high positions of authority in the world of financial governance. They have argued that the financial sector has grown too big, that many of its activities have little, or even negative social value, and that the productivity and efficiency of the world economy could be improved in the financial sector were to shrink. Lord Adair Turner, former Chairman of the UK's FSA remarked in an interview with Prospect Magazine and then in a speech in September, 2009: "…" …not all financial innovation is valuable, not all trading plays a useful role, and that a bigger financial system is not necessarily a better one." (Turner, Mansion House Speech, 2009). Defending his Prospect Magazine remarks, he remarked: "…while the financial services industry performs many economically vital functions, and will continue to play a large and important role in London's economy, some financial activities which proliferated over the last ten years were 'socially useless', and some parts of the system were swollen beyond their optimal size." (ibid.)

Former Federal Reserve Chairman Paul Volcker reportedly told a room full of bankers:Top of FormBottom of Form "I wish someone would give me one shred of neutral evidence that financial innovation has led to economic growth — one shred of evidence". Nobel Prize winner, the late James Tobin, raised early concerns about the growth and social efficiency of the financial sector: James Tobin's important essay, "On the Efficiency of the Financial Sector" first published in Lloyd's Bank Review in 1984 defined four different types of financial system efficiency. Of the fourth concept Tobin writes: "The fourth concept relates….to the economic functions of the financial industries... These include: the pooling of risks and their allocation to those most able and willing to bear them... the facilitation of transactions by

[1] Thanks to James Crotty for many useful discussions and for his important contributions to this project, and to co-authors and research assistants Leila Davis, Arjun Jayadev, Iren Levina, Juan Montecino and Joao Paulo de Souza. Thanks also to Tom Palley for very helpful discussions. Finally, many thanks to INET and the Political Economy Research Institute (PERI) for financial support.

providing mechanisms and networks of payments; the mobilization of saving for investments in physical and human capital… and the allocation of saving to their more socially productive uses. I call efficiency in these respects functional efficiency". Tobin goes on to write: "I confess to an uneasy Physiocratic suspicion, perhaps unbecoming in an academic, that we are throwing more and more of our resources, including the cream of our youth, into financial activities remote from the production of goods and services, into activities that generate high private rewards disproportionate to their social productivity (Tobin, 1984 [1987])".

Indeed, one could do a back of the envelope calculation of the recent practices of the functional efficiency, to use Tobin's term, of the global financial system: When all is said and done, the global financial crisis – instigated by our banks, hedge funds, and other financial institutions – will cost the world economy in terms of lost jobs and economic output somewhere between 60 and 200 trillion dollars. That is from Andrew Haldane of the Bank of England (Haldane, 2010.) This is real money—and real lives.

We are living in a financialized capitalism, a capitalism where our large financial system has a major impact on our lives and livelihood (Palley, 2013). For several decades, this financialized capitalism has been locked in a devastating dynamic of de-regulation, financial innovation, financial crash, and government bail-out. Then the cycle starts over again with bailed out banks and bank CEO's and "rainmakers" more emboldened to lend more and take on more risks in the future. The result has been an ever expanding financial sector in many of the world's richest countries. In the United States, for example, the total financial assets have grown from four times the size of GDP in 1945 to 10 times GDP in 2008. This growth has been accompanied by a startling increase in profits in the financial sector in the US. By 2006, just before the crash, financial sector profits constituted a full 40% of all total domestic profits in the United States.

We have witnessed similarly large increases in the size and profitability of the financial sector in the UK and in several other European countries. Accompanying this massive increase in the size and profitability of finance has been a dramatic increase in inequality in the US, UK and some other heavily financialized economies. We have calculated a measure of the share of income accruing to the financial sector and to holders of financial assets: we call this the "rentier share" of income (Jayadev and Epstein, 2009). As Figure 1 shows, this rentier share has grown rapidly in the US since the 1980's, while labor income has grown much more slowly. Much of this growth in inequality in the US is due to the increase of the very top incomes and a lot of that increase is driven by financial incomes and the incomes of CEO's of major corporations. That raises the question of whether increased inequality is the price society must pay for a highly productive and socially useful financial sector? Let us see.

Figure 1. The Growth of Rentier Incomes vs. Labor Incomes in the US (1952 -2010)

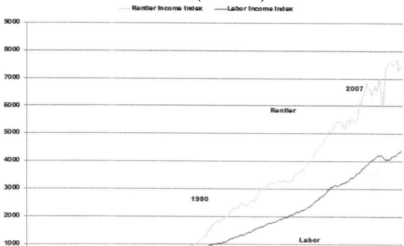

Source: Jayadev and Epstein

Figure 2. Financial Income and Economic Growth in the US, 1860 – 2010

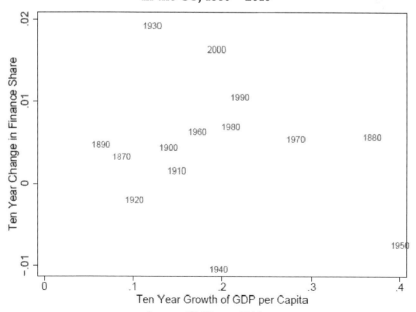

Source: Phillipon, 2011.

The contributions of finance to society: a closer look

What are the contributions of this massive financial sector to society? We have already seen that the massive costs of the current financial crisis bring into question the contributions of a massive financial sector. But perhaps over the long run, more finance contributes to more rapid economic growth. Could this be true?

Again, it is hard to find evidence of this result in the data. Figure 2 shows that, looking over a 150 year time span (1860-2010) in the US, there is no apparent relationship between the share of national income going to financial business and the rate of economic growth.

The absence of a clear connection between financial activity and positive economic outcomes, such as economic growth, is surprising. That is because a properly functioning financial system might be expected to contribute significantly to the health of the economy. As James Tobin suggested, the positive roles potentially played by the financial system include:

- Channeling finance to productive investment
- Providing mechanisms for households to transfer income over time
- Helping families and businesses to reduce risk (risk sharing)
- Helping provide stable and elastic LIQUIDITY to households and businesses
- Developing new, useful financial innovations.

So, if the financial system is fulfilling these functions, it should be leading to a healthier economy, should it not?

The puzzle is solved, however, when we look at how our actually existing financial system has been handling all of these important functions: and it's not a pretty picture.

Channeling finance to productive investment

The first and perhaps most important function of the financial sector is to mobilize and channel financial resources to productive investment, since productive investment is a key driver of employment and productivity growth in the economy. But as Table 1 indicates, in recent years, finance has been providing a decreasing share of the financial resources used by non-financial corporations in relation their capital investment needs. The so-called financing gap – the gap between investment resources needed and those available from corporate saving - has been going down in the US relative to the amount invested in capital equipment and factories (and this is also true of the UK and several other European countries).

Table 1. Financing gap relative to capital expenditures of non-financial business in the US, 1950 – 2009.

Average	1950-59	1960-69	1970-79	1980-89	1990-99	2000-09
	11.5%	12.5%	21.0%	11.2%	5.0%	-0.2%

Source: Author's calculations from Bureau of Economic Analysis Data

If the financial sector has not been lending as much as previously to non-financial corporations for investment, what have they been doing? One thing is they have lent large amounts to household in the build-up to the destructive housing and real estate bubbles in the US, UK and elsewhere. In addition, banks have simply been lending increasing amounts to each other as the financial sector has engaged in massive "proprietary trading" and gambling as they have tried to build up their income and bonus pools for their traders. Figures 3 and 4 show estimates of the share of lending by financial institutions to each other over the last fifty years.

Providing Mechanisms for Households to Transfer Income over Time and Helping families and businesses to reduce risk (risk sharing)

Nor has the financial sector performed well as a mechanism helping households save for retirement. For starters, the great financial crash of 2008 wiped out an estimated $16 trillion of household wealth in the US between 2007 -2009, of which only about 45% might have been restored since that time (Luttrell, et. al. 2013). The near zero interest rates fostered by central banks in the aftermath of the crisis has also significantly reduced the returns earned by savers in fixed income type securities. There is also evidence that the financial advising and management services industry that manages wealth in the US and elsewhere earns high management fees for relatively poor investment returns relative to much simpler self-designed financial strategies (Greenwood and Scharfstein, 2013). Furthermore, private pension funds have performed rather poorly for most Americans (Schultz, 2011). In short, the financial system has done a poor job of helping households provide for retirement.

Figure 3. Net lending of the financial sector to itself as a share of total net lending: UK, 1963 – 2012 (from 5% to 35% of lending

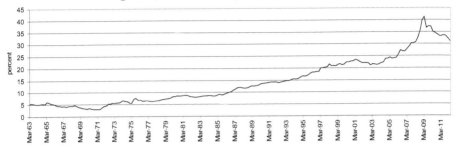

Source: Calculations based on data from Bank of England, Bankstats, Table A4.1. Data are not seasonally adjusted and include only sterling lending. Lending in foreign currencies is excluded

Figure 4. Financial sector lending to itself as a share of total lending: US, 1950 – 2010.

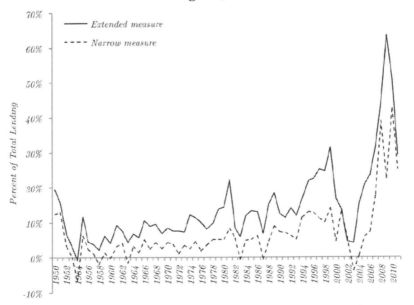

Source: Author's calculation based on the US Flow of Funds Accounts. The "narrow measure" is a safe "under-estimate" of intra-financial lending, and the "extended measure" is a more broad based measure which might be an over-estimate.

Helping provide a stable, elastic, and liquid credit supply to households and businesses

The financial crisis has clearly demonstrated the illusion of appropriate and stable credit provision by the financial system to households and businesses. In the build-up to the financial crisis the financial sector provided massive amounts of credit to households and businesses that fostered housing and real estate bubbles and to financial institutions that were bundling, packaging and selling off complex and ultimately toxic securities. But when the bubble burst and banks tried to dump as many of these dodgy securities as possible, liquidity in the market dried up as few buyers could be found for these questionable assets. As their values collapsed, banks tottered on the edge of bankruptcy, requiring bailouts from taxpayers, and then banks tightened credit conditions to protect their resources, drying up liquidity for households and businesses that were trying to refinance houses and maintain their businesses (Crotty and Epstein, 2014). In short, the current financial system has proven to be a poor provider of appropriate and predictable supplies of credit.

Developing new, useful financial innovations.

Financial innovations, such as collateralized debt obligations, were at the center of the financial crisis of 2007 – 2008 (Jarsulic, 2012). More generally, studies of financial innovations have been unable to find any connection between financial innovation and economic growth. As Crotty and Epstein show in a review of studies from the 1980's – 1990's, 30 – 40 percent of financial innovations in the U.S are undertaken for tax or regulatory avoidance rather than to reduce costs facing customers or enhancing the quality of the products for end users (Crotty and Epstein, 2009a). In short, these innovations simply redistribute the economic pie, rather than increase its size. Consequently, they are neither socially useful nor functionally efficient. Financial innovations offer a lot of promise but it appears that they deliver few positive results.

Restructuring finance to better serve society

For the past five years, politicians and regulators on both sides of the Atlantic have been promising regulatory reform to make finance safer and more socially efficient, but, so far, little has been accomplished. The financial lobbies on both sides of the Atlantic have been extremely effective at stalling and distorting anything but the most minimal improvements in financial regulations, despite important efforts by economists and other activists from organizations such as Americans for Financial Reform in the US and Finance Watch in Europe. The fight is not over, however, and a redoubling of effort on the part of reformers is necessary to improve the chances of positive change.

What reforms can help create more financial stability and also restructure finance to better serve society? Here is a list of suggestions culled from the work of these and other financial analysts (see also Crotty and Epstein, 2009b, and Epstein and Pollin, 2011):

1. Current policy, especially in Europe, has been focused on increasing capital requirements at banks. This could help but it will not be sufficient. Capital requirements, especially those based on risk weighting, can be easily gamed; and even in the best of circumstances, they contribute to the pro-cyclicality of the financial system: the value of capital goes up in the boom, giving banks more room to lend which, in turn, can derive up the asset bubble further.

2. Leverage requirements, as long as they are strict and defined in a way that is not pro-cyclical can be an important tool for limiting risks in the financial sector.

3. Policies to reduce the amount of speculative trading, such as financial transactions taxes, can be effective and the campaigns underway to institute such taxes in Europe and the   US should be strongly supported.

4. Reducing incentives facing financial actors – the traders and rainmakers of finance – to take on excessive risks is of critical importance. These reforms include, for example, limiting the payments to such actors, and forcing them to place a larger portion of these payments in escrow accounts for a period of time, so they can be clawed back if the financial investments sour.

5. Limiting the risk taking behavior by large financial firms, including splitting off their high risk activities from deposit taking and lending activities, should be implemented. The "Volcker Rule" was an attempt to implement such a plan, though it has been riddled with so many loopholes it might not be effective when implemented. The Vickers plan in the UK is designed to "ring fence" excessively risky activities by banks. Unfortunately, though heading in the right direction, these plans have to be strengthened considerably for them to be effective. And even these reinforced plans would not be effective unless large complex financial organizations are slimmed down, simplified and broken up to the point that they can be both managed and regulated properly (see point 6 below).

6. Phase out crisis driven bail-outs of financial firms. This would mean breaking up the too big to fail financial institutions so that the government could no longer be blackmailed into bailing them out and phasing out over time the implicit guarantees to bail out bankers.

Of course, it is likely to still be necessary for a "lender of last resort" to provide liquidity in case of a crisis, but there will be no need to bail out the bankers simply because their institutions are so large and interconnected that they would threaten the entire economy if they were to fail.

7. To reinforce points 5 and 6 above, government support of "finance without financiers" should be increased: that is, there should be more public support for public and cooperative financial institutions such as credit unions, cooperative banks, and public banks to fulfill the key roles of a properly functioning financial system as described by Tobin under the rubric of functional efficiency (Epstein, 2010).

This is, of course, only a partial list. But economists and activists working to improve the functioning of our financial systems on both sides of the Atlantic have a rich and sophisticated understanding of policies that need to be undertaken and could easily expand on and deepen these ideas. However, to implement these reforms the role of money in politics needs to be dramatically reduced so that the voices of reform can be heard. Moreover, given the transatlantic mobility of finance, transatlantic cooperation among reformers will also be required if we are to succeed in restructuring finance to better serve society.

References

Arcand, J-L, E Berkes, U Panizza (2011), "Too much Finance?" VoxEU.org, 7 April. http://www.voxeu.org/index.php?q=node/6328

Crotty, J. and Epstein, G. (2009a), "Controlling dangerous financial products through a financial pre-cautionary principle", *Ekonomiaz*, No. 72, 3rd Quarter, 2009, pp. 270 – 291.

Crotty, J. and Epstein, G. (2009b), "Avoiding another meltdown" in *Challenge Magazine*, January-February, 2009, pp. 5 – 26.

Crotty, J. and Epstein, G. (2013), "How big is too big? On the social efficiency of the financial sector in the United States?" in *Capitalism on Trial: Explorations in the Tradition of Thomas Weisskopf*, eds. Robert Pollin and Jeannette Wicks-Lim. Northampton, Ma: Edward Elgar Press.

Crotty, J. and Epstein, G. (2014), "The last refuge of scoundrels: Keynes-Minsky perspectives on the uses and abuses of the "Liquidity defense", in Gerald Epstein, Tom Schlesinger and Matias Vernengo, *Financial Institutions, Global Markets, and Financial Crisis: Essays in Honor of Jane Webb D'Arista*. Northampton: E. Elgar.

Epstein, G. (2010), "Finance without financiers: Prospects for radical change in financial governance: David Gordon memorial lecture" in *Review of Radical Political Economics*, 42 (3), September, pp.293 – 306.

Epstein, G. and Jayadev, A. (2005), "The rise of rentier incomes in OECD countries: Financialization, central bank policy and labor solidarity", in Gerald A. Epstein, ed. *Financialization and The World Economy*. Northampton, MA: E. Elgar Press, pp. 46 -76.

Epstein, G. and Pollin, R. (2011), "Regulating Wall Street: Exploring the political economy of the possible", Political Economy Research Institute, University Of Massachusetts, Amherst, MA.

Greenwood, R. and Scharfstein, D. (2013), "The growth of finance", *Journal of Economic Perspectives*, Spring, pp. 3 - 28.

Haldane, A. (2010), "The 100 billion dollar question" Bank of England, March.
http://www.bankofengland.co.uk/publications/speeches/2010/speech4 33.pdf

Haldane, A. and Madouros, V. (2011), "What is the contribution of the financial   sector,"   VoxEU.org,   22   November.
http://www.voxeu.org/index.php?q=node/7314

http://business.timesonline.co.uk/tol/business/industry_sectors/banking_an d_finance/article6949387.ece

Times of London (2009), "Wake up, gentlemen', world's top bankers warned by former Fed chairman Volcker" December 9.

Jarsulic, M. (2012), *Anatomy of a Financial Crisis A Real Estate Bubble, Runaway Credit Markets, and Regulatory Failure*, Palgrave Macmillan, December 2012.

Luttrell, T., Luttrell, D., Atkinson, T. and Rosenblum, H. (2013), "Assessing the costs and consequences of the 2007–09 financial crisis and its aftermath," Dallas Federal Reserve Economics Letter, September.

Palley, T. (2013), *Financialization; The Economics of Finance Capital Domination*, London: Palgrave MacMillan.

Philippon, T. (2011), "Has the financial sector become less efficient?" November.

Schultz, E. (2011), *Retirement Heist; How Companies Plunder and Profit from the Nest Eggs of American Workers*, New York: Portfolio/Penguin.

Tobin, J. (1984 [1987]). "On the efficiency of the financial sector", *Policies for Prosperity; Essays in a Keynesian Mode*, ed. Peter M. Jackson. Cambridge: MIT Press.

Turner, A. (2009), "Mansion House Speech", September, 22.
http://www.fsa.gov.uk/pages/Library/Communication/Speeches/2009/ 0922_at.shtml

12. The Financial System, Financialization and the Path to Economic Recovery

Damon Silvers, *Policy Director, AFL-CIO, Washington, DC, Dsilvers@aflcio.org.*

Introduction

One of the extraordinary intellectual consequences of the crisis that began in 2007, and which we are still in, is that it forced the economics profession to adjust its discourse on the question of whether there is a relationship at all between events in the financial system and macroeconomic outcomes. This is despite the fact that every financial regulatory change that has occurred in relation to finance in modern history in any country has been justified in political terms because of supposed positive impact on the real economy. At the same time, among academic economists, for the past thirty years the prevalent view was that financial markets had no impact on long-term real economic outcomes. Moreover, even after more than 40 trillion dollars in real economy losses, it has taken no less an authority than the IMF in its 2010 symposium to resolve that there is a connection.

But the connection is more than the obvious idea that financial crisis beget economic crises. The era of financialization is associated with deteriorating labor market conditions. This was true before the financial crisis that began in 2007, but since the financial crisis high unemployment has contributed to dramatically reduced labor force participation. Over the last generation, the US has become an increasingly financialized economy. Financial assets—which remained steady at between 400 and 500% of GDP during the period from 1960 to 1980, grew to over 1000% of GDP just prior to the crash of 2008. At the same time, the employment to population ratio fell from 80% in 1989 to less than 75% today. For men, the decline was particularly precipitous, falling from 90% in 1989 to less than 80% today.

Now that we understand the downside risk of inadequately regulated financial markets, the focus of policymakers on both sides of the Atlantic has been on addressing the risk of future systemic financial shocks. Far less attention has been devoted to the much more important questions of how to manage the consequences of the actual major financial bubble that just burst, and how in future to assure that financial markets and financial institutions play their proper intermediary role in a manner that contributes to sustainable growth and job creation, rather than merely to safely facilitating unproductive speculation.

While the solutions to the continuing economic crisis lie substantially in the area of fiscal, monetary and labor market policy, proper financial regulation and tax policy are important aspects of the policy approach needed for the world to emerge from the continuing economic crisis and enjoy a better future of shared and sustainable prosperity.   Furthermore, this is particularly important when one considers financialization as a phenomenon of political economy—with powerful effects not just on the functioning of financial markets and institutions themselves, but on the political possibilities of constructive fiscal, monetary, labor market and tax policy.

What is financialization?

At its heart, financialization is the rising dominance of secondary financial markets over other forms of economic activity. To understand the difference between financialization and the healthy functioning of a financial system, it is worth beginning with what a financial system is supposed to do. Financial systems, which include both financial markets and financial institutions, are supposed to transform savings into productive investments by allocating capital. The financial system plays a fundamentally intermediary function, and the goal of public policy should be to ensure that it does so efficiently and cost-effectively.

There are other forms of capital allocation and transformation of savings into investment. Operating firms engage in this activity constantly, as do households. Governments do so as well, and there is a great deal of evidence that a healthy economy requires government to engage in the process of capital allocation at a level necessary to supply the economy with necessary public goods.

To the extent the financial system engages in the transformation of savings into investment, it does so in primary capital markets—the issuance of equity and debt by operating companies and public institutions, the funding of student loans, the making of loans by banks to operating companies.

However, the vast majority of activity in the contemporary financial system occurs in secondary markets—the trading and lending of securities, derivatives, and other financial instruments. Financialization is the rising importance of secondary financial markets in the economic life of nations.

The public policy roots of financialization

Financialization in the last thirty years has its roots in both technological developments (e.g. the falling cost of executing financial transactions) and a set of conscious public policy choices. Those public policy choices began in the 1970's at a global level with the move toward floating currencies after the collapse of the Bretton Woods system, and then continued in the United States with the dismantling of the structural regulation of financial institutions. That process that began with the Garn-St. Germain Act in the early 1980's, and reached its culmination in the Gramm-Leach-Bliley Act of 1997 that repealed what remained of Glass-Steagall, allowing the essentially unregulated use of credit market institutions to fund securities and derivatives trading.

Similar processes occurred in other key secondary financial markets, including mortgage backed securities and derivatives. The deregulation of derivatives amounted to the deregulation of the institutional insurance market, as derivatives were largely used as a form of insurance.

Finally, tax policy explicitly encouraged financialization, as the United States lowered capital gains rates to levels well below that of wage income, and financial market transactions were exempted from the larger shift in revenue toward sales taxes and value added taxes.

The economic consequences of financialization

The resulting growth in the importance of secondary market activity in the US economy had two immediate and direct effects on the overall allocation of capital to productive investment. First, increasing amounts of savings were needed to support secondary market activity. This is best understood through the idea that every gambler needs a stake. Every hedge fund, every proprietary trading desk, every high speed trader needs capital in addition to the capital immediately at risk. This capital must be held in liquid, risk free assets—reducing the amount of savings available to invest in illiquid, risky activities—i.e. operating businesses.

Further, and more subtly, financialization affected the allocation of human capital. In the United States, secondary market activities have absorbed more and more human capital —particularly the type of human capital such as expertise in mathematics, electrical engineering, computer science, and physics, that is key to innovation and problem solving in the real economy.

Finally, and perhaps most importantly, financialization has led to the accumulation of wealth, and political power, by secondary market institutions, and the people who work for them and own them. This political power has been used to promote public policies that favor the interests of secondary market institutions (i.e. the interests of banks, stock brokers, money managers, etc.).

The failure of post-crisis responses to challenge financialization

Since the beginning of the crisis in 2007, we have seen the two issues of managing the consequences of the burst bubble and ensuring the financial system does its job in the future, badly mismanaged on both sides of the Atlantic. In many ways, the nature of the mismanagement seems to be distinct between the E.U. and the US, but really they share certain common key features.

In the aftermath of the crisis, US policy focused on maintaining the health of what had become a very over-concentrated financial sector, rather than repairing the financial health of households. While it is true that the Federal Reserve's policy of quantitative easing has reduced the cost of debt to both households and firms, direct balance sheet assistance from government, in the form of both equity and subsidized debt, was provided primarily to banks and not to households. Total outlays to banks in terms of equity and subsidized debt was measured in the trillions, whereas total assistance to households in the TARP was approximately $50 billion, most of which has been unspent.

In fact, US policymakers' approach to rescuing the financial sector, which was to dilute but not eliminate existing equity in the banks and make whole long term bank creditors, ensured that households would have to make good on obligations that were based on inflated bubble era values. The result has been a kind of debt peonage foisted on households, which have spent the last five years making payments on underwater bubble-era mortgages.

This approach has been so embedded in US policy since 2007 that it has been largely forgotten how great a departure this approach is from how the US handled the two prior significant banking crises since the creation of the Federal Reserve in 1913. Both of these major crises, the Great Depression and the Savings and Loan Crisis, were handled by the write down of inflated bank assets, the restructuring of bank balance sheets, and the offering of relief to bank borrowers.

In Europe, a similar dynamic has occurred regarding household debt in some member states, Ireland and Spain in particular. But the more important dynamic has involved the interaction between public debt and the banking sector. Looking through ideology and rhetoric, it is hard not to conclude that European policy responses since the beginning of the crisis, and particularly since 2010, have had the paramount goal of preserving the stability of the European banking system as an end in itself, with little thought as to what that would mean in terms of short and medium term macroeconomic outcomes.

Reversing financialization and fostering real economy growth

What would financial policy look like if it was actually oriented toward promoting long term sustainable growth in the real economy? It would seek to: 1) minimize the impact of the past—the debt overhang left by the bubble by restructuring both the debt itself and the banks, 2) promote availability of commercial credit for the real economy, 3) minimize the cost of financial intermediation to the real economy, 4) ensure adequate investment in public goods, and 5) minimize the impact of future bubbles on the credit system. Bubbles will always occur but they do not have to impact the credit system the way the housing bubble did.

The first goal requires somewhat different approaches in the US rather than Europe. In the US it requires principal reduction in home mortgage loans, with consequent restructuring of bank balance sheets that brings liquidity back to commercial credit markets. In Europe, the issue is the extent to which the ECB allows bondholders to manage European fiscal and monetary policy in the interests of creditors, as opposed to the interests of the broader economy as a whole and the public.

Since August, 2012, the ECB has come to understand that it is necessary at some level to counteract the bond market vigilantes. However, even though the ECB and the IMF are no longer allowing public creditors to have direct control over economic policy thru the bond market, they have substituted for that their own command and control mechanisms, which appear to be having a similar effect.

The remaining goals require a set of interlocking economic policy initiatives designed to foster sustainable, long-term, low cost financial intermediation. In other words returning the banking system as a kind of public utility, and not as a competitor to venture capital, as an arena of high risk, high return investment strategy, backed up by implicit public guarantees.

The key measures that would achieve this goal are:

- separation of commercial credit institutions from financial market-oriented institutions. In other words, the return of what in the US terms is called a Glass-Steagall type of banking regulation;
- A tax regime that ceases to subsidize speculative activity, in other words a financial transactions tax, and
- limiting the overall concentration in the financial system.

Putting the financial markets debate in a larger social context

A deeper question is embedded in debates over financial policy. That is the question of what exactly are we asking of financial markets and financial institutions? There is no question that financial markets provide a certain type of narrowly defined efficiency. How narrowly defined? The only part of the efficient capital market hypothesis that has survived the empirical tests of the last two decades is its weakest form, which is that past asset prices convey little information about how to make above market returns.

We have learned at great cost is that capital markets are not good at evaluating complex interlocking issues of political economy, technology or science. We also know with some certainty that private capital markets will not on their own allocate sufficient capital to public goods to produce sustained economic growth.

The financial transactions tax can be viewed as a policy solution to this problem. If the European Commission's assessment of its revenue potential is correct (understand the shift geographically here), the FTT has the potential to fund as much as half of the US's infrastructure deficit over the next 10 years if the US adopted the European proposal for the FTT. However, given the challenge of climate change and the global shift from wages to returns on capital, even a global FTT is not going to be enough to fund the world's public good needs.

Meeting global public good needs will require a much more significant globally coordinated approach to the taxation of returns on capital. It will also require an end to the toleration by the world's major economies of a global tax system effectively dominated by the existence of tax havens.

This challenge leads to a final point about financial concentration and political economy. While there have been European examples of concentrated financial systems paired with strong labor movements resulting in successful political economies, recent US experience suggests that a political economy dominated by concentrated universal financial institutions without a hegemonic labor movement is incapable of generating public policy outcomes in the public interest. Consequently, a political economy dominated by finance represents a fundamental threat to public support for democracy itself.

Polling conducted by a wide variety of independent sources over the last 5 years has shown that the American public supports, by wide margins, a set of obvious public policy initiatives needed for long-term sustained prosperity; accountability for the banks, including legal accountability for what they did to cause the financial crisis; progressive taxation; infrastructure investment; rebuilding of US manufacturing capacity; and protecting our social insurance system as a primary public policy objective.

Each of these issues impacts jobs and growth, and polls more than 70% support among the American public. Yet, not only are these steps not being taken in Washington, they are largely outside of the mainstream of Washington policy discussion. This disconnection between the public and governing elites over economic policy, and in particular, over the treatment of the banks, is a key causal factor in the present dysfunctionality of American politics. Behind this disconnection is the power of finance, which speaks to the importance of a financialization reform agenda, not only for the economy, but for democracy too.

13. Delays, Dilutions, and Delusions: Implementing the Dodd-Frank Act

Jennifer Taub, *Associate Professor, Vermont Law School, South Royalton, Vermont, jtaub@vermontlaw.edu.*

The post-crisis commitment to financial reform

Five years ago, the Lehman Brothers bankruptcy filing triggered a run on the shadow banking system, leading to cascading collapses here and abroad (D'Arista & Epstein, 2010). Credit markets froze, the stock market plummeted, residential real estate prices fell, and unemployment climbed to double digits. More than four million homes were lost to foreclosure (Blomquist, 2012). What started as a banking crisis stemming from the use of excess short-term leverage to finance high-risk mortgage-linked securities (Taub, 2011), became an economic crisis and the largest downturn since the Great Depression (FCIC, 2011).

Members of the Bush administration (Paulson, 2008) made the promise of "never again" to justify the extraordinary government interventions to bail out and shore up the very institutions whose risky practices caused the collapse. The promise that the government would prevent future crashes was what helped Bush convince Congress to support the $700 billion Troubled Asset Relief Program, one small piece of the multi-trillion dollar bailout (Herszenhorn, 2008). Members of the Obama administration echoed this promise of never again, assuring the public that if their vision of reform legislation passed, the government would never again bail out the banks (McCarthy, 2010).

The Obama administration's reform vision was set out in a white paper (US Treasury, 2009) and later became a central part of the Dodd-Frank Act aimed at eliminating or reducing the conditions that caused the crisis. And, the "never again" promise also softened the public's ire. For example, in the summer of 2009 at a televised forum moderated by PBS news anchor Jim Lehrer, Federal Reserve Chairman Ben Bernanke defended the bailouts drawing upon both fear and promise. He explained:

"So, it wasn't to help the big firms that we intervened. It was to stabilize the financial system and protect the entire global economy. Now, you might ask . . .Why are we doing that? It's a terrible problem. It's a problem called a too-big-to-fail problem. These companies have turned out to be too big to allow to collapse because . . .when the elephant falls down, all the grass gets crushed as well." (Bernanke, 2009)

Additionally, Bernanke said: "We really need - and this is critically important - we really need a new regulatory framework that will make sure that we do not have this problem in the future." This type of statement was made to address to the growing sense that banks got a soft landing when the housing bubble burst, whereas ordinary people faced the rough justice of the marketplace. President Bush implicitly admitted this when he said he "abandoned free-market principles to save the free-market system," (Runningen and Hughes, 2008). But such a double standard could be rationalized only if it was presented as absolutely essential and if the future did not look the same. Absent that, President Bush's rescue would have been tantamount to saving a system that trampled ordinary Americans while propping up the elephants -- the privileged bank executives, their large shareholders and creditors.

The stymieing of reform

Yet, today, the elephants are larger and the grass is still crushed. The top banks are bigger and still borrow excessively in the short-term and overnight markets leaving them vulnerable to large scale, sudden runs. Whereas at the end of 2006, the top six bank holding companies had assets equivalent to 55 percent of GDP (Johnson, 2011), at the end of the second quarter of 2013 their assets were equivalent to 58 percent (National Information Center, 2013 and BEA, 2013). While banks have increased their equity capital slightly, and there are calls by regulators and reformers for even higher requirements, their legal obligation is merely three percent of total non-risk-weighted assets. That allows borrowing of $97 for every $100 in assets, or a 33-1 leverage ratio. Such levels of leverage were a key factor in the 2007 - 2008 crisis (Admati, DeMarzo, Hellwig & Pfleiderer, 2011), yet both permitted and actual leverage still remains far too high (Admati 2013). Experts like former FDIC Chair Sheila Bair call for a minimum of eight percent (Bair, 2012), and others, such as finance scholars Anat Admati and Martin Hellwig suggest between twenty to thirty percent (Admati & Hellwig, 2013) to help ensure banks internalize, not socialize their losses.

In addition to size and leverage, banks are still dangerously interconnected and prone to wholesale runs due to their excessive dependence on short-term, often overnight borrowing through the repurchase agreement (repo) market. Repos are collateralized loans, often made by cash-rich financial entities (including money market mutual funds) to others who use the money to finance their balance sheets. Because billions of dollars can be pulled back by a repo lender the next morning, these transactions made banks (including Bear Stearns and Lehman) vulnerable to runs by other banks and financial entities (Copeland, Martin & Walker, 2011). Indeed the crisis peaked with "a run on repo" (Gorton, 2009). Lehman, for example, had $200 billion outstanding in overnight repo loans before it collapsed (Sandler, 2011). One mutual fund family that had been rolling over $12 billion in overnight loans to Lehman, suddenly demanded its money and tapered down its overnight repo loans to just $2 billion a week later (Sandler, 2011). At the peak, in spring of 2008, about $2.8 trillion in collateral was posted through the tri-party repo market (Copeland, Martin & Walker, 2011). Today, repos remain a fragile source of funding (Lew, 2013), with roughly $1.8 trillion in collateral financed through just the tri-party repo segment of the repo market in July 2013 (New York Fed, 2013).

Many experts agree that the dangerous pre-crisis conditions persist (Konczal, 2013). Where there is a dispute is why and how we got here, and the implications. Some ask for our patience (Lew, 2013), hoping that full implementation of the Dodd-Frank Act will deliver on the "never again" promise set out in its preamble: "To promote the financial stability of the United States by improving accountability and transparency in the financial system, to end 'too big to fail', [and] to protect the American taxpayer by ending bailouts (Dodd-Frank, 2010)." Others insist additional Congressional action is necessary. Those who believe waiting will yield insufficient results include several former bankers, current community bankers, and regulators who contend it is time to proactive break up the largest banks (American Banker, 2013). Some experts advocate for additional steps to reduce banks' dependency on overnight and other very short-term financing (Hoenig & Morris, 2011). However, there are others who advocate for less regulation, not more, and hope to repeal Dodd-Frank. They argue the answer is to allow what they call the "free market" to cure the problem (Allison, 2013).

How did it happen?

How did this happen? We can find the clues if we return to that same 2009 televised forum. Bernanke described what was set out in the Obama administration's white paper for reform, a document released just a month earlier. This, and some additional measures discussed below, would make up the financial stability portions of the Dodd-Frank Act. And, that is part of the problem. Bernanke described what would be done to "make sure we do not have this problem in the future." He explained:

> "[T]he present administration has proposed a system that would include - let me just mention two items. First, that the Federal Reserve would oversee all these major big firms that are, quote, "too big to fail," and would put extra tough requirements on their

capital and their activities, what they can do, the risks they can take.
. . But the second part is very important. We would modify the
bankruptcy code . . .[because] when one of these firms fails, it's a
disorderly mess. What we need is a system where the government
can say, this firm is about to fail, we can't let it just fail, but we've
got to - we don't want - also we don't want to prop it up either. We
need an alternative between bailout and bankruptcy, and that
alternative is a system where the government can come in and seize
the firm and then unwind it in an orderly way, sell off the assets,
and do that in a way that does not cause chaos in the financial
markets." (Bernanke, 2009)

The first element became part of the Dodd-Frank Act in the form of Fed
supervision of the largest bank holding companies and certain non-bank
financial firms (Dodd-Frank, 2013). The second also became part of the law
in the form of granting a new "orderly resolution authority" to the FDIC
(Dodd-Frank, 2013). Instead of preemptive downsizing and risk reduction,
these two measures aimed at stabilizing and preserving the existing system
became the centerpiece of the financial stability portions of Dodd-Frank.
That, in combination with strenuous industry lobbying to prevent stronger
measures from becoming part of the law, explains why we are where we are
today.

While there is great potential in Fed supervision, and the Fed has the
skills, knowledge and data to require the largest bank holding companies and
systemically important financial institutions to hew to enhanced prudential
standards, this has not yet been done. Moreover, thus far, proposals
describing what regulation will look like are far too weak.

For example, Section 165 calls for heightened prudential standards for
bank holding companies with $50 billion or more in assets (and also certain
nonbanks supervised by the Fed), and Section 166 calls for "early
remediation" (Dodd-Frank 2013) of such a firm, up to and including
management changes and asset sales. Under 166, the Fed is supposed to take
early remediation action if such a firm experiences "increasing financial
distress, in order to minimize the probability that the company will become
insolvent and the potential harm of such insolvency to the financial stability
of the United States." The Fed is required to make rules that establish
requirements for early remediation. However, the law itself hampers the Fed's
ability to be tough. Under Section 165(j), a firm that the Financial Stability
Oversight Council considers a "grave threat" is permitted to have a debt-to-
equity ratio of 15 to 1, in other words, equity capital of not much more than
six percent of total assets. This is less equity than sensible experts believe
should be required of a giant bank under normal conditions.

In addition, though the orderly liquidation authority is helpful for intervention, it cannot do all of the work. Furthermore the authority was weakened in the legislative process. Most notably, the obligation that banks pre-fund the process was taken out, so that now the taxpayers, via a line of credit from the Treasury will front the financing of the new process (Dodd-Frank, 2010). Again, while it is an important component, it cannot be the only safety measure. An emergency room is an essential facility, but deliberately running in front of moving cars is ill advised. The concept as described by Bernanke and embedded in the law is to intervene when a firm "is about to fail." This is too late.

The problem is that stronger proposed prevention measures were deleted or weakened before the law was enacted. The cutting room floor is littered with language that would have better targeted the actual conditions that caused the crisis. If enacted, by now, the largest banks would have been smaller and less risky. These include the Brown-Kaufman SAFE Banking Act (Dayen, 2010) and the McCain-Cantwell attempt to restore the Glass-Steagall separation of securities operations from deposit-taking. Even as Republican members of Congress were decrying having the industry pre-fund the FDIC for its orderly liquidation authority, claiming it was a bailout, they and many Democrats voted against Brown-Kaufman. Another important tool left out of the law included an amendment introduce by Senator Bill Nelson to end the special treatment repo lenders receive in bankruptcy, a reform designed to reduce systemic risk. (Lubben, 2010).

Furthermore, one of the strongest prevention measures that made it in to the statute, the Volcker Rule (Section 619 of the Dodd-Frank Act), has been delayed. The Volcker Rule limits the ability of banking entities that have access to FDIC deposit insurance or the Federal Reserve discount window to also engage in certain high risk trading and other speculative practices. This part of Dodd-Frank precludes them (subject to exceptions) from owning or sponsoring hedge funds and private equity funds. It also forbids them from trading for their own accounts. The banks object to this rule (Hopkins, 2012) even though they are using insured customer deposits to take tremendous risks which can pay off, but can also result in massive losses as illustrated by the case of JPMorgan Chase's London Whale trades.

By mid-2013, in addition to regulators, members of congress, former leaders of too-big-to-fail banks, current community bankers, academics and the public, banking analysts were joining the chorus of those who contended the largest banks should be downsized—however, in this instance, not because of the system's safety, but their own value (Touryalai, 2013). Yet, it is critical that reforms not only address size and leverage, but also focus on short-term funding through the wholesale lending markets, including tri-party repo to fund risky assets. Even top bankers testified this was a critical concern. For instance, at a Financial Crisis Inquiry Commission hearing in 2010, Goldman Sachs CEO Lloyd Blankfein noted:

> "Certainly, enhanced capital requirements in general will reduce systemic risk. But we should not overlook liquidity. If a significant portion of an institution's assets are impaired and illiquid and its funding is relying on short-term borrowing, low leverage will not be much comfort." (Blankfein, 2010).

Lastly, there is also need to decide on what the public's role should be regarding insuring deposits and backstopping the noninsured liabilities of banking and shadow banking institutions. This requires a more rigorous review of interconnections and a clear look at the role of regulated entities and private pools of capital across the globe. It is good that hedge fund advisers now need to register with the Securities and Exchange Commission, but it is time to consider restrictions on leverage and on short-term funding throughout the system. The combination of leverage and reliance on short-term funding is a tinderbox that could be easily ignited by an asset price reversal or some other shock.

References

Admati, A.R., DeMarzo, P.M., Hellwig, M.F., and Pfleiderer, P., (2011),"Fallacies, Irrelevant Facts, and Myths in the Discussion of Capital Regulation: Why Bank Equity is Not Expensive," Working Paper 86, Rock Center for Corporate Governance at Stanford University, p. 8.

Admati, A and Hellwig, M. (2013), *The Bankers' New Clothes: What's Wrong with Banking and What to Do about It, Princeton*, NJ: Princeton University Press, pp. 4 - 5, 7-8, 182.

Admati, A.R. (2013), "We're All Still Hostages to the Big Banks," *New York Times*, August 25, 2013.

Allison, J.A. (2012), "The Cure for the Banking Industry, Part IV, Why Dodd-Frank is No Help," *The American Banker*, September 27.

American Banker (2013), "Who Else Wants to Break Up the Banks," slideshow, available at http://www.americanbanker.com/gallery/too-big-too-fail-breaking-up-big-banks-1048735-1.html

Bair, S. (2012), *Bull by the Horns: Fighting to Save Main Street from Wall Street and Wall Street from Itself*, New York, NY: Free Press, pp. 325 - 326.

Barofsky, N. (2012), *Bailout: An Inside Account of How Washington Abandoned Main Street While Rescuing Wall Street*, New York, NY: Free Press.

Bernanke, B.S. (2009), PBS NewsHour forum in Kansas City, MO. Transcript available at http://www.pbs.org/newshour/bb/business/july-dec09/bernanke_07-27.html

Blankfein, L. (2010), The Official Transcript of the First Public Hearing of the Financial Crisis Inquiry Commission Hearing, January 13, p. 9.

Blomquist, D. (2012), "2012 Foreclosure Market Outlook," RealtyTrac.com, available at http://www.realtytrac.com/content/news-and-opinion/slideshow-2012-foreclosure-market-outlook-7021

Bureau of Economic Analysis (2013), Press Release, National Income and Product Accounts, Gross Domestic Product, 2nd quarter 2013 (second estimate); Corporate Profits, 2nd quarter 2013 (preliminary estimate), available at http://www.bea.gov/newsreleases/national/gdp/gdpnewsrelease.htm

Copeland, A., Martin, A., and Walker, M. (2011), "Repo Runs: Evidence from the Tri-Party Repo Market," Federal Reserve Bank of New York Staff Report No. 506, Revised in 2012, pp. 1, 9.

D'Arista, J. and Epstein, G. (2010), "Dodd-Frank and the Regulation of Dangerous Financial Interconnectedness," in Will It Work? How Will We Know? The Future of Financial Reform, The Roosevelt Institute.

Dayen, D. (2010), "Brown Kaufman Introduce the Safe Banking Act of 2010," Firedoglake, April 21, available at http://news.firedoglake.com/2010/04/21/brown-kaufman-introduce-the-safe-banking-act-of-2010/

The Dodd-Frank Wall Street Reform and Consumer Protection Act of 2010, Public Law 111-203, Preamble and Title I, Title II, Section 619.

Federal Reserve Bank of New York (2013), Daily Average Collateral Value Financed in the Tri-Party Repo Market, available at http://www.newyorkfed.org/banking/pdf/daily_avg_size_tpr_jul2013.pdf

Financial Crisis Inquiry Report: Final Report of the National Commission on the Causes of the Financial and Economic Crisis in the United States (2011), Official Government Edition (the FCIC Report).

Gorton, G. (2009), "Slapped in the Face by the Invisible Hand: Banking and the Panic of 2007," Yale and NBER, Prepared for the Federal Reserve Bank of Atlanta's 2009 Financial Markets Conference: Financial Innovation and Crisis, May 11-13, p. 30, 33 - 34.

Herszenhorn, D. (2008), "Bailout Plan Wins Approval: Democrats Vow Tighter Rules," *New York Times*.

Hoenig, T.M. and Morris, C.S., (2011), " revised in 2012, "Restructuring the Banking System to Improve Safety and Soundness," pp. 28 - 29, available at http://www.fdic.gov/about/learn/board/Restructuring-the-Banking-System-05-24-11.pdf

Hopkins, C. 2012, " US Banks to Make Another Push Against Volcker Rule," Bloomberg, December 13.

Johnson, S. (2011), "Tunnel Vision or Worse from Banking Regulators," New York Times Economix, available at http://economix.blogs.nytimes.com/2011/01/20/tunnel-vision-or-worse-from-banking-regulators/

Konczal, M. (2013), "Does Dodd-Frank Work? We Asked 16 Experts to Find Out," Washington Post WonkBlog, July 20, available at http://www.washingtonpost.com/blogs/wonkblog/wp/2013/07/20/does-dodd-frank-work-we-asked-16-experts-to-find-out/

Lew, J. (2013), Testimony before the Senate Committee on Banking, Housing, and Urban Affairs Hearing on the "The Financial Stability Oversight Council Annual Report to Congress," including prepared remarks and Q&A, May 21.

Lubben, S. (2010), "The Bankruptcy Code Without Safer Harbors" *American Bankruptcy Law Journal*.

McCarthy, M. (2010), "Geithner: If Reform Passes, Government Will Never Again Bail Out Banks," ABCnews.go.com.

National Information Center (2013). Top 50 Holding Companies Summary Page, available at http://www.ffiec.gov/nicpubweb/nicweb/Top50Form.aspx

Paulson, H.M. (2008), Remarks at the Ronald Reagan Presidential Library. Simi Valley, California, available at http://www.treasury.gov/press-center/press-releases/Pages/hp1285.aspx.

Runningen, R. and Hughes, J. (2008), "Bush Considers Options for GM, Chrysler Rescue Plan," Bloomberg.com.

Sandler, L., "Lehman Had $200 Billion in Overnight Repos Pre-Failure," Bloomberg, January 28.

Taub, J.S. (2010), "A Whiff of Repo 105," The Baseline Scenario, March 16, available at http://baselinescenario.com/2010/03/16/a-whiff-of-repo-105/

Taub, J.S. (2011), "The Sophisticated Investor and the Global Financial Crisis," in Corporate Governance Failures: The Role of Institutional Investors in the Global Financial Crisis, Philadelphia, PA: University of Pennsylvania Press, 188 - 216.

Tourlayai, H. (2013), "Split Up JPMorgan Chase And Value Jumps $59B: Analyst," Forbes.Com, August 23, available at http://www.forbes.com/sites/halahtouryalai/2013/08/23/jpmorgan-chase-value-jumps-by-59b-if-broken-up-analyst/

US Department of the Treasury (2009), Financial Regulatory Reform -- A New Foundation: Rebuilding Financial Supervision and Regulation, available at http://www.treasury.gov/initiatives/Documents/FinalReport_web.pdf

14. Risky or Safe? Government Bonds in the Euro Area Crisis

Silke Tober, *Macroeconomic Policy Institute (IMK), Hans Böckler Foundation, Dusseldorf, Germany, silke-tober@boeckler.de.*

Safe-asset quality: the neglected issue

The financial crisis of 2008/2009 showed the tremendous damage financial market turbulence can cause to the real economy. The collapse of confidence in the banking system, the partial interruption of financing, and the bleak economic outlook caused GDP in 2009 to decline by 3.1% in the United States, by 5.1% in Germany and by 4.4% in the euro area as a whole. Four years later, in June 2013, unemployment was still at 7.6% in the United States and 12% in the euro area, while unemployment in the most troubled euro area economies of Spain and Greece was above 26% and youth unemployment was 56% and 63%, respectively.[1]

It is now widely accepted that more regulation of financial markets is needed and, although many reform proposals appear to have been discarded along the way, some reforms are underway. Basel III, for example, increases capital ratios and, very importantly, is likely to introduce a maximum leverage ratio for banks. The Single Supervisory Mechanism for banks in the euro area is also a step forward, as is the Dodd-Frank Act in the United States.

However, there is one issue in the euro area that has not been tackled at all and has actually been aggravated by recent regulation. That issue is restoring to government securities the quality of "safe assets". Dealing with this issue is essential for getting the euro area out of the current financial and economic crisis and eliminating one important source of future financial instability.

"Safe" assets are assets that are as close to being risk-free as one can get in the real world. They are an important feature of developed economies, because they add stability, being a reliable store of value and an important component in the regulation of banks as well as serving as benchmarks for pricing other assets and as collateral (International Monetary Fund 2012).

Government bonds are the classic "safe asset"; not by decree, but because of the special status of the issuer. This special status of governments

---

[1] Unless otherwise noted, the source for economic data is Eurostat and the AMECO database, last updated 3 May 2013, the source for monetary data are the national central banks of the Euro system and the ECB.

emanates from two factors. First, governments unlike other economic agents can favorably affect the economic environment by implementing prudent macroeconomic policies. Second, government debt is ultimately backed by the entire national economy as the government has the authority to collect taxes. Furthermore, the national central bank can act as market maker in the case of slackening demand for national government securities.

The status of government securities as safe assets implies that risk premiums are low or absent and thus interest rates are relatively low, which is a big plus for tax payers. The yield on ten-year government bonds in Japan averaged only 0.9% in June 2013 even though gross government debt is expected to reach 244% of GDP in 2013. US government bonds with a remaining maturity of ten years carried a relatively low yield of 2.3% despite a debt ratio of 111% (2013).

Figure 1. 10-year government bond yields of selected euro area countries. (daily, in %)

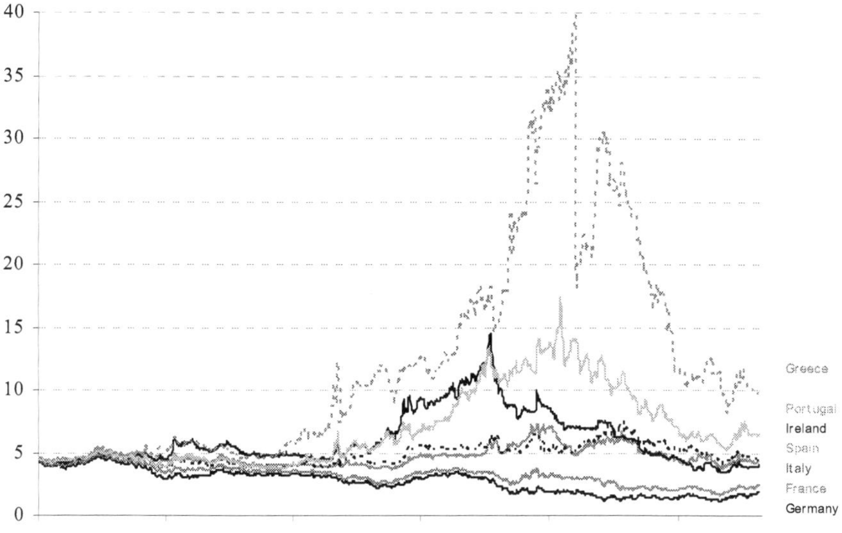

Source: Reuters EcoWin (EcoWin Financial).

In the euro area, by contrast, government securities of only some countries are now viewed as "safe", whereas others carry high risk premiums (see Figure 1). As a result, interest rates in these countries are high not only for newly issued and existing government debt, but for the entire national economy with adverse effects on growth and employment. Since early 2010 more and more countries have been pulled into the vicious cycle of elevated perceived risk, increased interest rates, low growth or even recession, and a worsening financial situation of the government (i.e. rising budget deficits and mounting debt). The vicious cycle has been fueled by fiscal austerity and deterioration of bank balance sheets. As fiscal policy became more restrictive in response to rising budget deficits the economy was further depressed. Bank balance sheets, already weakened by problem assets accumulated prior to the financial crisis, deteriorated further because of both the decline in the price of government securities and the faltering economy.

Safe-asset quality ill-advisedly forsaken

Had the government securities of Greece, Ireland, Italy, Portugal and Spain not lost their safe-asset status, an important propelling force of the current crisis, if not the most important one, would not have materialized. The European Stability and Growth Pact might still have compelled the countries of the euro area to undertake fiscal consolidation but expansionary monetary policy could have provided an effective counterweight and the negative economic outlook stifling investment would not have taken hold.

As it is, high risk premiums seriously impaired the transmission mechanism of monetary policy. Elevated interest rates and credit crunches continue to constrain domestic activity in many countries of the euro area.

So why did euro-area policy makers do nothing to counter the loss of confidence in government securities? The principal reason seems to have been a fear of evoking moral hazard. The reasoning was that it had been profligate spending that had gotten the troubled euro area countries into a mess, and these countries needed to do "their homework" and clean up their act by themselves. If they were not punished for their misdeeds, but instead bailed-out by other countries, a dam would open to unleash a flood of unchecked government spending.

This reasoning was flawed on at least two accounts. First, excessive government spending was not the cause of the current crisis. Second, given the institutional set-up of the euro area, the countries concerned were simply not able to resolve their problems alone.

Take Spain, for example: between 1999 and 2007, when the international financial crisis erupted, Spain had reduced its government debt ratio from 62% to 36% of GDP and in all but one year would have satisfied even the strict fiscal deficit target of the Fiscal Compact, adopted by the euro area countries in 2012.[2] Similarly, Ireland reduced its public debt ratio from 47% of GDP in 1999 to 25% of GDP in 2007. The European Commission and euro governments criticized neither Spain nor Ireland, nor even Cyprus, for their national "business model" until their economies started spiraling

---

[2] This is the case from a real time perspective, which is the relevant one, when evaluating whether policy targets are met. Ex post, structural deficits have been revised upward substantially in line with the downward revision of potential output estimates.

downwards. Yet today, they are reprimanded for fiscal irresponsibility, bad business models and, in the case of Cyprus, money laundering.

In the majority of the now troubled euro area countries it was private rather than public debt that caused imbalances to mount. Growth rates were high and unit labor costs increased in excess of the European Central Bank's inflation target of 1.9%. At the same time other countries of the euro area, notably Germany, experienced low growth rates that depressed import demand and stagnating unit labor costs that increased the price competitiveness of German firms. Current account imbalances built up over a period of nine years but were largely ignored because of the narrow focus policy makers had on fiscal deficits.

When the crisis hit, these countries were not able to devalue their currencies nor did they have a central bank willing to stave off the speculative attack against their bonds.

From the beginning, the cornerstones of the crisis resolution strategy in the euro area were fiscal austerity and emergency loans as a last resort. This strategy was institutionalized by the Fiscal Compact with its focus on balanced budgets and debt reduction, and by the European Stability Mechanism (ESM) which provides loans to troubled countries contingent on compliance with adjustment programs. The depressing economic effects of austerity were viewed as collateral damage that was part of the process of regaining the trust of financial investors. Furthermore, the distrust of investors, as mirrored in yield differentials within the euro area, was seen as an instrument to discipline governments in their insatiable desire to spend money (The same reasoning caused euro governments to attach the prohibitively high rate of 5.5% to the initial emergency loans extended to Greece in 2010.)

However, the international financial crisis clearly shows that financial markets react late and exhibit herd behavior. Instead of being a disciplinary force, a loss of investor confidence can trap a country in a vicious cycle of higher financing needs, austerity measures, declining growth, a further loss of confidence, and banking troubles. Chancellor Merkel's insistence on private sector involvement caused the first wave of contagion in October 2010. The announcement of a write-down of privately held Greek government bonds led to a new peak in yields and the spreading of the confidence crisis to Spain and Italy in the summer of 2011.

Similarly, the ESM treaty is likely to undermine the safe-asset quality of government securities and increase the risk of future speculative attacks by prescribing government bonds to carry collective action clauses that regulate private sector involvement in case of payment difficulties. Collective action clauses are usually only included in foreign-currency government bonds because they carry exchange rate risk and the government might not be able to attain the foreign currency necessary to service its foreign-currency debt.

However, euro area countries are now adopting this practice for bonds denominated in the currency that they collect as taxes.

Had euro governments jointly guaranteed Greece's government debt in early 2010 they would in all likelihood have managed to nip the crisis in the bud. In 2010, Greece's government debt amounted to 329.5 billion euros or 3.6% of the euro area's GDP. All that was needed was a willingness to guarantee that sum so as to keep interest rates low and create favorable conditions for Greece to service and repay this public debt. Instead the crisis deepened and spread, pulling in country after country.

ECB: Between a rock and a hard place

The lack of decisive action on the part of governments put the European Central Bank (ECB) in a difficult position. On the one hand, the ECB had to come to the rescue repeatedly to prevent a severe financial crisis and break-up of the euro area; on the other, the ECB could not launch a full-fledged stabilization effort – whether it wanted to or not – because governments had proclaimed government bonds to be risky assets and a central bank simply does not have the mandate to risk large amounts of tax payer money (Tober 2013).

Aware of the dangers of further eroding investors' confidence, time and again the ECB declared that Greece was solvent, opposed calls for debt rescheduling or haircuts, and called upon the governments to act (Draghi 2011; ECB 2011; The Economist 2010). In May 2010, the Euro system[3] began to intervene in bond markets to prop up Greek, Irish and Portuguese government bonds. Owing to lack of government backing, the focus of monetary policy then shifted from stabilizing government bond markets to stabilizing the no-less-risky banking sector. The Euro system significantly increased its refinancing and emergency loans to banks. The level peaked in late June 2012 at 1447 billion euros, a three-fold increase compared to the pre-crisis level in mid-2007. 70 percent of these refinancing loans went to Greece, Ireland, Italy, Portugal and Spain, which in 2007 had accounted for only 15 percent of the total. By this time, the Euro system had already suspended its government bond purchase program with a maximum volume of 219 billion euros in early March 2012.

The enormous refinancing need of banks in troubled euro countries resulted largely from capital flight as private investors divested their financial assets from these countries. Correspondingly, the arrears between the euro

---

[3] The Euro system comprises the European Central Bank and the national central banks of the euro area.

area's national central banks increased in almost equal magnitude,[4] showing the extent to which the ECB's attempts to forestall a collapse of the euro area allowed private investors to shift their risks to the public sector. The Target2 liabilities of Greece, Ireland, Italy, Portugal and Spain reached almost 1000 billion euros in the summer of 2012, while Germany had corresponding assets of above 700 billion euros.

In September 2012 the ECB announced its willingness to purchase government bonds in unlimited amount, provided the troubled country would engage in an ESM program. Already in late July, ECB president Mario Draghi had famously vowed to do whatever it takes "to preserve the euro", adding "and believe me, it will be enough" (Draghi 2012). And yes, within its mandate the ECB is in principal able to do what it takes to put an end to this crisis, but only if euro area governments tow the same line. Once governments decide to do everything it takes to preserve the euro, the ECB would not only be able to act but would actually be legally obliged to do so, unless this were to cause a conflict with the ECB's primary mandate of maintaining price stability (EU 2010).[5]

Quick fix: Debt Redemption Fund

Regaining investor confidence is a necessary condition for steering the euro area economy back to high employment and high productivity growth. The initial strategy of harsh fiscal austerity backfired because it deepened the recession, reducing confidence rather than strengthening it. By contrast, a joint guarantee of euro area government debt could immediately restore safe-asset status to government securities. With investor confidence restored, not only would yields on government bonds decline, so too would those on bonds issued by non-financial enterprises and credit institutions. Bank balance sheets would improve as declining risk premiums cause government bond prices to increase. Combined with improved prospects for the economy, confidence would also return to the banking system. The excessive central bank refinancing of credit institutions would vanish, as would the Target2 balances.

A joint and several liability of euro area sovereign debt could be realized by setting up a temporary debt redemption fund. Such a fund was first

---

[4] These assets and liabilities between national central banks of the Euro system result from cross-border transactions and are transformed into arrears vis-à-vis the ECB at the end of each day. They are called Target2 assets and liabilities because of the name of the interbank payment system in the euro area: Trans-European Automated Real-time Gross Settlement Express Transfer System.

[5] "Without prejudice to the objective of price stability, it shall support the general economic policies in the Union with a view to contributing to the achievement of the objectives of the Union as laid down in Article 3 of the Treaty on European Union." (EU 2010, Article 2)

proposed by Vincenzo Visco and the German Council of Economic Experts (SVR 2011, Parello/Visco 2012). The euro area countries would jointly guarantee all euro area government debt in excess of 60% of the respective national GDP, which would then be repaid over a period of 25 or 30 years. Each country would service its own debt. The schedule of debt repayment would be independent of the remaining maturity, so any debt falling due would be refinanced unless it happened to coincide with the repayment schedule.

There is nothing magical or economically expedient about a debt ratio of 60%. It just happens to be the level deemed adequate when the euro area was conceived, being the level debt converges to if nominal growth is 5% and the fiscal deficit ratio 3% of GDP. It would also be the convergence ratio if nominal growth is only minimally above 3.3% and the fiscal deficit ratio is at 2 %. Given an initial level of 80% and a fiscal deficit of 1.5%, the debt ratio of a country with 3.3% nominal growth would converge to 60% within 30 years. If the initial debt ratio is 100%, the fiscal deficit would have to be 1% to reach 60% within 30 years.

The examples show that the reduction in the debt ratio – and thus repayment to the debt redemption fund – would result mainly from growth and, in most cases, would even allow for fiscal deficits, albeit small ones. Given large output gaps, vigorous growth is to be expected in the first years after a debt redemption fund is established. This would enable the troubled countries to balance their budgets. Repayment to the fund would commence a couple of years after the fund is established and installments made dependent on cyclical factors. Countries could, for example, commit to a specific path for non-cyclical government expenditure that brings the debt ratio down to 60% of GDP within the required time frame, given assumptions about average nominal growth.

The situation of Greece is the most difficult: four years into the euro crisis and after six years of deep recession, Greece's debt ratio of 175% (2013) exceeds its level in 2009 by 45 percentage points, despite the reduction of privately held debt by 53% in March 2012.

Temporary tax increases on high incomes and wealth would increase the fiscal room for maneuver. Not only do they seem warranted in the case of Greece, they also seem warranted in countries like Germany where the debt ratio increased by nearly 20 percentage points during the global financial crisis. It seems reasonable that the main burden be borne by those who can shoulder it most easily and likely profited most from the state assistance given to banks.

Urged by the European Parliament, the EU Commission recently launched a group of experts to assess the feasibility of a debt redemption fund (EU Commission 2013). The main point of contention is likely to be moral hazard. However, this problem may be overstated. The euro area crisis was caused by flaws in its institutional architecture, especially a misguided early warning system, not by profligate government spending. It was also greatly aggravated by the global financial crisis. The focus of macroeconomic surveillance has now widened to include unit labor costs, inflation and current account balances. At this stage, gearing policies towards low unemployment, adequate growth, and low inflation, should actually lower the risk that individual countries will pursue self-serving national strategies to the detriment of other member states.

References

Draghi, Mario (2011): Continuity, consistency and credibility. Introductory remarks by Mario Draghi, President of the ECB, at the 21st Frankfurt European Banking Congress "The Big Shift", Frankfurt am Main, 18 November 2011

Draghi, Mario (2012), Speech by Mario Draghi, President of the European Central Bank at the Global Investment Conference in London 26 July 2012.

ECB (2011), Private Sector Involvement and its Financial Stability Implications, European Central Bank, Monthly Bulletin, October, p. 159-161.

EU Commission (2013), President Barroso, in agreement with Vice-President Rehn, launches Expert Group on debt redemption fund and euro. MEMO/13/635, 2 July 2013.

EU (2010), Protocol (No 4) on the Statute of the European System of Central Banks and of the ECB, Official Journal of the European Union, C 83/230, 30.3.2010.

European Central Bank (2012), Cyclical Adjustment of the Government Budget Balance. In: Monthly Bulletin, March 2012. p. 102ff.

German Council of Economic Experts (2011), Stable Architecture for Europe – Need for Action in Germany. Annual Report 2011/12, Wiesbaden.

Horn, Gustav A. et al. (2010), Reforming the European Stability and Growth Pact: Public Debt is Not the Only Factor, Private Debt Counts as Well. IMK Report, Nr. 51e, July 2010.

International Monetary Fund (2012), Safe Assets – Financial System Cornerstone? Global Financial Stability Report, April, p. 81 – 122.

Parello, C. P.; Visco, V. (2012), The European Redemption Fund: A Comparison of two proposals. MPRA Paper No. 42874.

The Economist (2010), Game, set and match to Angela. Charlemagne's notebook, Euro-zone governance, 29 October 2010.

Tober, S. (2013), "Reluctant Lone Ranger – The ECB in the Euro Area Crisis," in *The Social Dimension of the Economic Crisis in Europe*, edited by Heinz Stapf-Finé. June: 9 – 28.

15. Transatlantic Trade Partnership Versus Transatlantic Currency Cooperation

Jan Priewe, *Professor of economics at HTW Berlin – University of Applied Sciences, Germany, Jan.Priewe@htw-berlin.de.*

Introduction

In spring 2013 the US government made a proposal for negotiations with the European Union (EU) for a Transatlantic Trade and Investment Partnership (TTIP). The EU commission and most EU governments applauded, and some media reported high prospective growth and trade effects for both the US and EU-27. Amazingly, except for a recent plea from French President Francois Hollande to consider measures to reduce exchange rate volatility, nothing has been proposed for currency cooperation between the Federal Reserve (Fed) and the European Central Bank (ECB).

This essay argues that President Hollande's idea is much more promising than TTIP. Unfortunately, questioning the rationality of foreign exchange markets is taboo on both sides of the Atlantic. That taboo constitutes a major obstacle to policy advance and prevents the US and Europe from enjoying the benefits that would flow from sensible currency cooperation.

Meagre dividends from TTIP

Average tariff rates in the US and in the EU range around 3 to 4% for industrial goods, and for agricultural commodities they are 13.9% (EU) and 5% (US) (Mildner and Schmucker 2013). Consequently, except in those few special product groups where tariffs are substantially higher, lowering tariff barriers to trade will have very small effects.

Non-tariff barriers are widespread and linked to entrenched standards, norms and subsidies, related to sector policies such as agriculture or pharmaceutical industry or food, and protective rules in public procurement. Abandoning them or going for mutual acknowledgement involves a host of contentious issues. Rules for foreign investment, be it foreign direct investments (FDI) or financial investments, touch on sensitive issues, and dismantling these rules could in some cases be similar to financial deregulation.

Francois et al. (2013) estimate maximum benefits from TTIP for the year 2027 at 119 bn Euro for the EU and 95 bn Euro for the US. That amounts to around 0.9% and 0.8% of 2012 GDP for the EU and US respectively. This increase in GDP would be distributed over many years, but long-run growth rates would be unchanged. If the gestation period were ten years, there would be a temporary increase in GDP growth of less than 0.1 percentage points which then fades away. The bottom line is the macroeconomic impact on GDP growth is almost negligible – the debate is a storm in a teacup from a macroeconomic point of view.

These observations do not speak against TTIP. They merely demonstrate that in a period of low growth one should not expect TTIP to be an economic stimulus program. Furthermore, TTIP is bilateral trade negotiation and bilateral agreements also generate trade diversion, which is costly. At a systemic level, they also undermine the multilateral trading system.

Trade with the US is also not large enough to yield significant benefits from marginal bilateral trade liberalization. In 2012, EU imports from the US were 4.5% of total imports (intra-EU trade plus extra-trade with non-EU countries[1]) or 11.5% of all EU-27 extra-trade imports (data from Stephan and Löbbing 2013). This share has fallen significantly since the inception of the Euro 1999. In 2012 EU-27 exports to the US were 6.5% of total exports and 17.3% of EU-27 extra-trade exports. With regard to Europe's total trade (exports plus imports), the US constitutes 5.5% of total trade and 14.3% of total EU-27 extra-trade. For Germany, the US is only the 4th most important trading partner after France, Netherlands and China.

These numbers raise the question of why the transatlantic trade is so small and why its share is falling. Moreover, the traded value-added would be even smaller since many exports are produced with imports from other countries. 62% of EU-27 trade is intra-EU trade, and much of this is intra-euro-area trade. The predominance of intra-EU trade may be caused, to some extent, by a common currency and the more or less pegged exchange rates with the majority of the ten non-euro EU-members. There is widespread consensus that a monetary union, equivalent to irreversibly tight exchange rates, spurs trade. Rose (2000) estimated that monetary unions triple trade within a union. The implication is that greater exchange rate stability across the Atlantic could increase transatlantic trade, perhaps by even more than TTIP.

Transatlantic currency cooperation

The possible benefits from exchange rate stabilization between the euro and the dollar are manifold: lower transaction costs, more and intensified trade, reduced inflationary impulses during depreciation episodes, more balanced

---

[1] Intra-trade is the trade between the 27 members of the EU; extra-trade is the trade of the EU with the rest of the world.

current accounts contributing to contemporaneous internal and external macroeconomic equilibrium; and reduced current account imbalances.

Currency cooperation might also start to transform the global currency "non-system" of floating exchange rates into a new and more stable order of currencies. If competition between the two reserve currencies is reduced and more cooperation between the Fed and the ECB in monetary policies were achieved, real effective exchange rates (REER)[2] for the rest of the world could become more stable. This would help developing and emerging economies to cope better with financial globalization since they are hit harder by exchange rate volatility.

These potential benefits are contested by mainstream opinion which still holds that there is no robust empirical evidence that exchange rate volatility harms trade or incites currency crises. Instead, it is asserted that companies and financial systems can cope with volatility if macroeconomic policies are appropriate. Mainstream economists also claim that persistent over- or undervaluation of exchange rates is unlikely unless policy enforces imprudent rigid pegging.

Numerous empirical studies have generated inconclusive results so that mainstream opinion, particularly at the ECB and Deutsche Bundesbank, is that freely floating exchange rates are the best of all worlds. The US government and the Fed also subscribe to this view, albeit less vehemently. The bottom line is that it is taboo on both sides of the Atlantic to question this "Frankfurt-London-Washington" dogma which is based on assertion and lacks robust empirical evidence.

That this policy view is so dominant is amazing since it is also implicitly questioned by many mainstream economists. Short-term, and perhaps even medium-term, forecasts of exchange are impossible (Meese and Rogoff 1983). Volatility of floating exchanges cannot really be explained: the main candidate, Dornbusch's overshooting model, fails empirically (Rogoff, 2003). There is insufficient proof that in the long run the purchasing-power-parity-theory of exchange rates holds, even though the opposite is repeatedly asserted (Rogoff, 1999; Isard, 2007; Chinn, 2008) and these assertions contradict the undisputed evidence that deviation from purchasing-power-parity equilibrium is strong and pervasive. The efficient market hypothesis does not apply to foreign exchange markets, and exchange rate formation is more and more influenced by ultra-short term algo-trading, herding and noise-traders with no concern about fundamentals. These findings imply that there is no discernible exchange rate equilibrium in the reality of pure floating. If the conclusion from all this is that there is no evidence that floating exchange rates are harmful, then it implies that equilibrium exchange rates

---

[2] Average nominal exchange rates to all trading partners, weighted with trade shares, and adjusted for inflation differentials.

don't matter. However, nobody believes that, especially in a globalized world economy, which means exchange rate volatility and concomitant temporary or lasting exchange rate misalignments are indeed damaging.

After the end of the Bretton Woods currency system of fixed exchange rates against the US dollar, European currencies moved to a freely floating exchange rate regime. The one period of exception was that of the Plaza and Louvre Accords between 1985 and 1987, when G5 governments agreed to use foreign exchange interventions to first depreciate the dollar and appreciate the Yen and the Deutsch Mark (DM), and then to halt the dollar's depreciation in 1987.

This floating regime led to huge volatility of G5 exchange rates. However, that volatility was mitigated between European currencies by three separate initiatives: the "currency snake" arrangement between 1972 and 1979; the European Monetary System (EMS) between 1979 and 1999; and the adoption of the euro 1999. The next section provides evidence on the extent of this volatility.

Dollar-Euro exchange rate volatility

Figure 1 shows the history of the US dollar – DM exchange rate (annual averages). After the end of the Bretton Woods arrangement the DM, then the leading anchor currency in Europe, rose in value against the dollar by 115% through the end of the 1970s. It then fell 38% between 1980 and 1985 in face of major interest rate increases by the Federal Reserve. Thereafter, the DM appreciated by 105% through to 1995, dropped by 35% through to 2001, and the rose again by 64% until the financial crisis 2008. Volatility, if measured by intra-year peaks and lows, has been much higher under both the DM and the euro regimes.

Figure 1. Nominal exchange rates of the D M/E urp vis à vis US -$, 1950-2012 (annual averages)

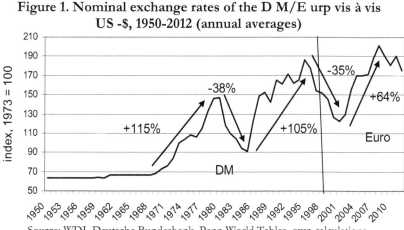

Source: WDI, Deutsche Bundesbank, Penn World Tables, own calculations.

For trade, the real exchange rate is more relevant than the nominal rate. Apart from the 1970s, inflation rates between the US and Germany or the Euro area have not differed much. Hence, as shown in Figure 2, real exchange rate volatility has been roughly the same as nominal exchange rate volatility. Since inflation has been similar, changes in the real exchange rate have had virtually nothing to do with differential cost changes between the two regions.

For Germany, an appreciation of the DM or euro in real terms of 105% is equivalent to a temporary mammoth export duty and import subsidy. Alternatively, it is equivalent to a massive increase in real wages in Germany compared to the US. Volatility on such a grand scale must inevitably distort trade. All economists would regard such export duties or subsidies or such wage increases (or drops) as hazardous and intolerable for the performance of output and employment. It is therefore amazing that they suspend judgment on real exchange rate variation of this magnitude.

Figure 2. Real exchange rate of the DM/€ against the US-$ 1973-2011 (annual values based on GDP deflators)

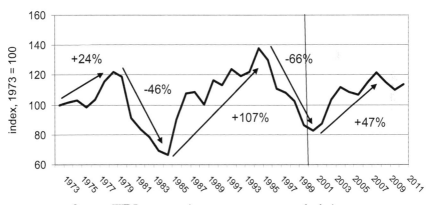

Source: WDI, www.nationmaster.com, own calculations.

As shown in Table 1, the absolute annual real and nominal exchange rate change (irrespective of plus or minus signs) in the period 1990-2013 was 8%; the monthly nominal change was 2.2%, and the swing between peak and low relative to the mean was around 66%.

Table 1. Volatility of monthly nominal exchange rates and the real exchange rate (RER) of DM and € against US -$1990-2013

	median	standard deviation	standard deviation, % of median	Monthly/ annual change (absolute value), %	peak	low	swing, % of median	swing/ standard deviation
Nominal exchange rate DM or €/1 US-$, monthly values	1.59	0.23	14.69	2.18	2.29	1.23	66.0	4.6
RER DM/€, annual values	108.2	15.7	14.5	8.1	137.7	66.4	65.8	4.5

Source: IMF, IFS, Oanda (online); own calculations, 1990-99 DM calculated in €

One reason why so many mainstream economists ignore exchange rate fluctuations may be that real exchange rates seem to move cyclically, occasionally passing points of purchasing-power-parity (PPP) (see Figure 3). That feature of occasionally equaling the purchasing-power-parity exchange rate deflects attention from the massive swings that have produced deviations as large as 30 and 40 percent under- or overvaluation relative to PPP for Germany, and even more than 80% for the Yen. Nonetheless, Figure 3 is somewhat misleading. That is because companies and sectors that lose competitiveness in face of strong appreciation may go out of business, which transfers their market shares to foreign companies. Consequently, their production is no longer counted statistically which alters the calculated PPP exchange rate. Production adjusts to exchange rates, not exchange rates to production (reverse causation). Recorded PPP-rates therefore undervalue the true deviation of price levels from PPP.

Figure 3. Conversion factor: PPP-exchange rates (GDP) to market exchange rates for selected OECD-countries 1980-2011

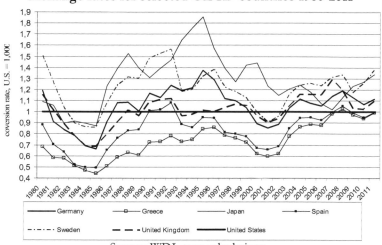

Source: WDI, own calculations.

Causes and effects of exchange rate volatility

98 percent of floating exchange rate transactions are attributable to capital flows, including exchange rate arbitrage and speculation. Short-term and ultra-short-term flows predominate. The foreign exchange (forex) markets, and particularly the Euro-dollar market, are by far the biggest global financial markets. The main drivers of forex transactions are expected yield differentials, changes in liquidity preferences, changing valuations of country risk premiums, diversification of assets and expected GDP growth in specific countries. Forex markets are expectation-driven and expectations are often inter-dependent so that there is no stable gravitation centre. The main reason exchange rates do not trend in one direction forever is because turnarounds are induced by central banks' monetary policies or by outright currency crises. Additionally, turnarounds may be induced by the interplay of destabilizing and stabilizing speculation which produces large overshooting swings but no stable "normal" exchange rate.

There are several mechanisms by which countries and companies cope with such swings but they are costly (cp. Clark et al. 2004):

- Exports can be denominated in foreign currency and hedged with forward contracts or with foreign exchange futures, for short periods up to a year. This raises transaction costs which are passed through on prices.
- Companies can diversify exports to different regions that use different currencies to reduce risk exposure.
- If companies manage to export and import inputs of intermediate goods in the same currency they can reduce adverse exchange rate repercussions.
- Companies engaging significantly in international trade also often transform themselves into transnational and multi-currency companies.
- Appreciation pressure can be passed on to suppress wages, while depreciation profits are not shared symmetrically with employees.
- Foreign direct investment can also mitigate exchange rate issues, but it replaces trade with foreign production.

Transnational corporations which "financialize" via hedging and exchange rate speculation, and which also have greater financial strength, are better positioned to cope with exchange rate volatility than small and medium enterprises. That means countries with less prevalence of transnational companies are disadvantaged in coping with volatile exchange rates. That is particularly true for developing and weaker developed countries. Taking all the arguments together, it comes as no surprise that intra-trade in the EU is so much deeper than extra trade given the far smaller exchange rate volatility between European currencies.

The harmful trade effects of exchange rate volatility are only part of the story. Another part concerns investment. Sunk costs, in the form of fixed investment, cannot be hedged. In the extreme case, capital may be entirely lost in face of large appreciation of the currency. Volatile exchange rates with cyclical swings amplify cyclical production instability. This causes booms and busts which often lead to current account imbalances and currency crises, especially for emerging economies. Chronic misalignments, in the form of overvalued exchange rates for some countries, suppress growth and employment or lead to over-indebtedness. The US-dollar has been structurally overvalued for many years, which has contributed to deindustrialization of the US economy. This in turn has contributed to high fiscal deficits geared to offset the private sector's lack of international competitiveness.

"Target zones" and exchange rates coordination

The idea of exchange targeting was proposed by John Williamson (1985) and Paul Krugman (1991). They advocate intermediate exchange rate regimes with neither fully fixed nor fully floating exchange rates. Williamson argues that the real effective exchange rates should be close to a fundamental equilibrium (FEER – fundamental effective exchange rate) which limits current account imbalances to around three percent of GDP. FEERs are to be calculated, agreed upon, and implemented via cooperative foreign exchange interventions orchestrated by central banks. Such a regime would be similar to managed floating and it could also have a reference rate band of +/- 10%.

The FEER system might work as follows. First a general consensus between the Federal Reserve and ECB and the respective governments is needed for containing bilateral exchange rate swings. Next, a bilateral real exchange rate close to purchasing power parity for tradables should be identified as the candidate for equilibrium.[3] The respective nominal bilateral exchange rate is then derived by the inflation differential. Thereafter, fluctuation bands are determined. Finally, the mode of mutual interventions must be determined, and here it is recommended that responsibility for intervention lie with the country whose currency is appreciating as it has unlimited supplies of its money to intervene with (Palley, 2003). Intramarginal interventions are advisable. Credible announcements of the central bank may suffice to deter speculators and guide markets.

---

[3] To include current-account-related goals is not sensible when dealing with a bilateral exchange rate. Even PPP-based effective exchange rates would not automatically balance the current account.

Such an arrangement would change the exchange rate regime from one of freely floating to one of coordinated managed floating. Interventions can also be sterilized on a discretionary basis and depending on the nature of inflation risks.

A target exchange rate regime for the two reserve currencies can mitigate currency competition and use the power of both currencies to contribute to greater global exchange rate stability. And once in place, it is likely that other key currencies would want to join. A critical function of a credible target exchange rate regime is leadership for expectations. This can mitigate speculation and herding and guide exchange rates toward the target. Intervention policies could be supported by a Tobin tax on foreign exchange transaction in the Euro-dollar markets, possibly at variable rates. Regulations to limit or even ban certain transactions with foreign exchange derivatives may also be desirable.

Lastly, there is also need for monetary policy coordination. Sterilized interventions can affect interest rates at the short end. However, large policy rate swings should be avoided in order to avoid interest rate induced exchange rate swings such as happened with the dollar in the early 1980s and the DM the early 1990s. This implies that fiscal policy should also be enlisted to fight inflation via a prudent mix of monetary and fiscal policy. Symmetrically, fiscal policy could also play a more active expansionary role in times of slump or recession compared to the present policy assignment that relies mainly on monetary policy. A prudent policy mix would reduce interest rate swings over the course of the business cycle, thereby also damp asset price fluctuations, and produce global economic gains by reducing global exchange rate and interest rate volatility.

The above approach would signal a new view whereby the global economy's two leading central banks recognize they have a *de facto* global impact for which they take responsibility. The benefits of this system of exchange rate coordination for the US and EU would likely dwarf the expected benefits of the TTIP.

References

Chinn, M.D. (2008), "Real exchange rates", in Durlauf, S., Blume, L.E. (2008), *The New Palgrave Dictionary of Economics*, 2nd edition, online.

Clark, P., et al. (2004), "A new look at exchange rate volatility and trade flows - some new evidence", IMF, Occasional Paper 235. Washington, DC

Francois, J., et al. (2013), "Reducing transatlantic barriers to trade and investment. An economic assessment", CEPR, London.

IMF (2013), IFS (International Financial Statistics), CD ROM. Washington, DC

Isard, P. (2007), "Equilibrium exchange rates: Assessment methodologies", IMF Working Paper WP/07/296. Washington DC

Krugman, P. (1991), "Target zones and exchange rate dynamics", *Quarterly Journal of Economics*, 106/3, 669-682.

Meese, R.A. and Rogoff, K. (1983), "Empirical exchange rate models of the seventies: Do they fit out of sample?" *Journal of International Economics*, 14, 3-24.

Mildner, S.-A., Schmucker, C. (2013): Abkommen mit Nebenwirkungen? Die EU und die USA stehen vor Verhandlungen über eine Transatlantische Handels- und Investitionspartnerschaft. SWP-Aktuell 26. Berlin.

Palley, T.I. (2003), "The Economics of Exchange Rates and the Dollarization Debate: The Case Against Extremes," *International Journal of Political Economy*, 33 (Spring), 61 – 82.

Rogoff, K. (1999), "Monetary models of dollar/yen/euro nominal exchange rates: Dead or undead," *Economic Journal*, 109(November), F655-F659.

Rose, A.K. (2000), "One Currency, One Market: The Effect of Common Currencies on Trade," *Economic Journal*, April, 9-45.

Stephan, S., Löbbing, J. (2013), Außenhandel der EU-27. Eine regionale und sektorale Analyse. IMK-Report 83, June. Düsseldorf.

WDI (2013), World Development Indicators (World Bank online).

Williamson, J. (1985), The Exchange Rate System. Washington: Institute for International Economics, Washington, DC

Williamson, J. (1987), "Exchange Rate Management. The Role of Target Zones," *American Economic Review*, 77, 200-204.

Williamson, J. (2004), "The dollar/euro exchange rate," *International Economics*, 4, 51-60.

IV
Labor Markets For Shared Prosperity

16. The Indispensability of Full Employment for Shared Prosperity[1]

John Schmitt, *Senior Economist*, *Center for Economic and Policy Research*, *Washington, DC, schmitt@cepr.net*

Challenging the conventional wisdom about unemployment.

The public debate about the state of the economy often frames equality and employment as inherently in conflict. According to the current politically dominant view, the only reliable way to create more jobs is to increase inequality: the claim is that lowering wages for workers at the middle and the bottom will make it profitable for firms to hire more workers.

This brief essay leaves the important broader critique of the inequality-unemployment trade-off to others[2] and seeks, instead, to highlight a different causal connection between inequality and unemployment: high unemployment increases inequality.

The focus is on the experience of the United States, which, by most measures, has the highest levels of --and has seen the biggest increases in-- inequality among the world's rich countries. Despite frequent references in the 1990s to the "Great America Jobs Machine," the United States has operated below even conservative estimates of full employment for most of the last three decades. That is, unemployment has been unnecessarily high in the United States precisely during the period when economic disparities have been on the rise.

The contrast between the path of inequality when unemployment rates have been low (as they were in the boom of the late 1990s) and when they have been high (as they have been during and since the Great Recession) suggests a strong link between high unemployment and increasing economic inequality. The strong macroeconomic performance of the late 1990s stands out, in particular, as a period with much to teach us today as the world economy continues to struggle from the lasting effects of the Great Recession.

To make the case for the importance of full employment, I will first demonstrate just how consistently the United States has strayed in recent decades from maximizing its output. I will then contrast the behavior of

---

[1] I thank Dean Baker, Jared Bernstein, Tom Palley, and participants at the February and March 2013 conferences on "A Trans-Atlantic Agenda for Shared Prosperity," sponsored by the AFL-CIO, the Friedrich Ebert Foundation, and IMK, for many helpful comments and discussions.
[2] For a critical summary of the debate, see David Howell (ed.), *Fighting Unemployment: The Limits of Free Market Orthodoxy*, Oxford University Press, 2004.

several indicators of inequality across two distinct periods --the boom of the late 1990s (1996-2000) and the bust of the late 2000s (2007-2009). Finally, I will draw some lessons about macroeconomic policy based on the experience of the second half of the 1990s.

Figure 1. Full Employment Gap, United States, 1949-2012

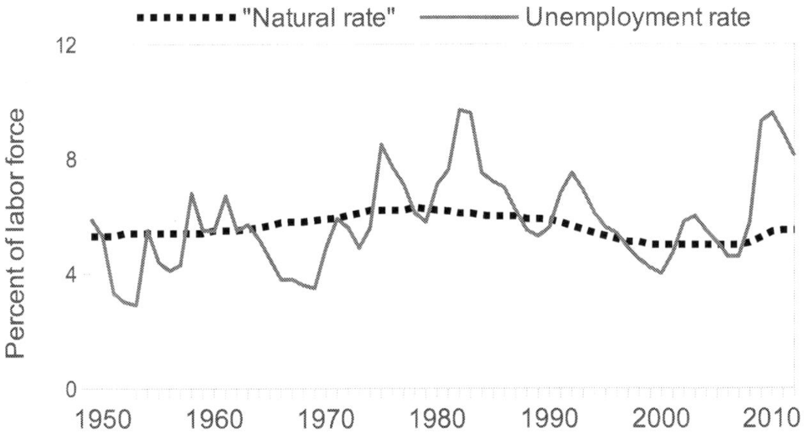

Source: Analysis of CBO, BLS data

Far from full employment

Since the end of the 1970s, the US economy has consistently failed to reach even fairly conservative estimates of full employment. Figure 1 shows the Congressional Budget Office's calculation of the "natural rate" (also sometimes referred to by the closely associated term "non-accelerating inflation rate of unemployment" or NAIRU) along with the official unemployment rate for the period 1949 - 2012. From 1949 through 1978, a period when economic inequality in the United States fell by most measures, the unemployment rate was at or below the CBO's natural rate in 21 of 30 years. During these same years, when the unemployment rate was above the natural rate, the difference tended to be small and short-lived. By contrast, from 1979 through 2012, the unemployment rate was above the full employment rate in 23 of the 34 years. Furthermore, in bad times the unemployment rate was much farther above the natural rate than the unemployment rate was below the natural rate in good times. In fact, if we weight the years above and below the natural rate by how many percentage points the actual unemployment rate diverged from the natural rate, between 1979 and 2012, the US economy experienced 36.1 unemployment-years when unemployment was above the natural rate, compared to only 5.4 years when unemployment was below the natural rate.

Inequality in booms and busts

Economists, sociologists, and social psychologists have documented the enormous costs of unemployment, whether measured in terms of lost economic output, the impact on disadvantaged communities, or physical and mental health.[3] However, academic and policy debates have underplayed the role that high unemployment has played in increasing inequality. While a comprehensive review of this connection is beyond the scope of this chapter, a few examples from recent economic history illustrate the size and strength of the connection between unemployment and inequality.[4] To make the point as simply as possible, let's compare how indicators of inequality behaved in two recent periods: the first, during the economic boom from 1995 through 2000, and the second, the recession and weak recovery from 2007 through 2010. In these boom years, unemployment averaged 4.6 percent, compared to 8.2 percent in the later bust. In the upswing, the unemployment rate fell 1.6 percentage points and employment rates increased 1.5 percentage points; in the downturn, unemployment soared 5.0 percentage points and employment dropped 4.5 percentage points.

The impact of unemployment on inequality is immediately obvious in Figure 2. In the low-unemployment years of the late 1990s, real family incomes grew faster at the bottom (the 20th percentile) than at the middle (the 40th and 60th percentiles) and almost as fast as the upper middle (80th percentile). Incomes did grow even faster near the top (95th percentile), but the contrast with the bust is striking. In the aftermath of the Great Recession, incomes fell at all levels, but most at the bottom, less in the middle, and least at the top. The low unemployment of the late 1990s was good for families at the bottom --and almost equalizing. The high unemployment of the late 2000s was bad for families across the board, but especially bad for those at the middle and the bottom, who fell even farther behind.

---

[3] For recent reviews of the private and public costs of unemployment, see Lauren Appelbaum (ed.), *Reconnecting to Work: Policies to Mitigate Long-Term Unemployment and Its Consequences*, Kalamazoo, Michigan: W.E. Upjohn Institute, 2012, and, Till von Wachter, Testimony before the Joint Economic Committee of US Congress on "Long-Term Unemployment: Causes, Consequences and Solutions," April 29, 2010, http://www.columbia.edu/~vw2112/testimony_JEC_vonWachter_29April2010.pdf
[4] For a thorough discussion of these issues, see Dean Baker and Jared Bernstein, *Getting Back to Full Employment: A Better Bargain for Working People*, Washington, DC: Center for Economic and Policy Research, 2013, available at http://deanbaker.net/books/getting-back-to-full-employment.htm.

Figure 2. Change in real family income by percentile

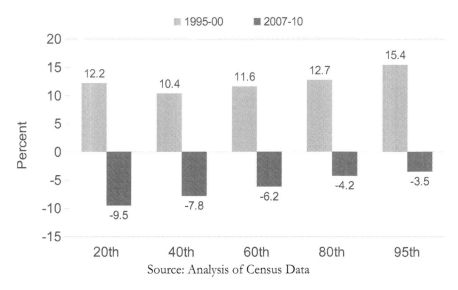

Source: Analysis of Census Data

A similar pattern holds for poverty rates by race in Figure 3. In the 1990s boom, poverty rates plummeted for racial minorities: down 4.7 percentage points for Asian Americans, 6.8 percentage points for African Americans, and 8.8 percentage points for Latinos, compared to a much smaller 1.1 percentage-point drop for whites. In the current bust, poverty rates rose least for whites (up 1.7 percentage points), more for Asian Americans (up 1.9 percentage points), and most more for blacks (up 2.9 percentage points) and Latinos (up 5.1 percentage points).

Part of these differences across booms and busts reflects the greater availability of work in upswings than in downturns. But part of the differences also reflects the increased bargaining power for workers at the middle and the bottom. When the unemployment rate remains low for a prolonged period, employers find it harder and harder to recruit and retain workers to meet high levels of demand for the goods and services they produce (when the unemployment rate is low, aggregate demand in the economy tends to be high). Under those circumstances, workers can ask for higher wages, better benefits, more flexible schedules, and other improvements in working conditions, and employers have little choice but to accede if they want to meet customer demand.

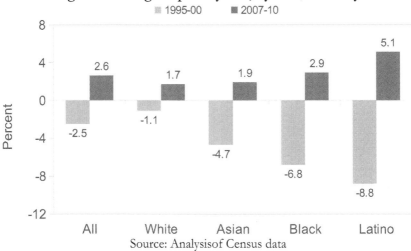

Figure 3: Change in poverty rate, by race/ethnicity

Source: Analysisof Census data

High unemployment has the opposite effect. Employers have little trouble finding and retaining workers, so workers reduce their demands regarding wages and working conditions. Over most of the last three decades, excessive unemployment rates have reinforced the pervasive decline in bargaining power set in motion by a host of other changes in economic policy. These other politically driven policy changes include the erosion of the inflation-adjusted value of the minimum wage, the fall in unionization rates in the private sector, the deregulation of many well-paying industries, the privatization of many state and local government jobs, the passage of pro-corporate trade deals, the creation and maintenance of highly dysfunctional immigration system, and other, related institutional changes that had as their primary effect the reduction of the bargaining power of workers at the middle and bottom of the wage distribution.

Macroeconomic Policy Lessons

Before and even into the early part of the 1995-2000 boom, the consensus of the economic profession in the United States was that the natural rate of unemployment was between 6.0 and 6.5 percent. Even many economists now widely known for the left-of-center views, including Paul Krugman, subscribed to this view.[1] One obvious lesson of the late 1990s boom was clearly that economists' methods for estimating full employment were too conservative.

---

[1] See, for example, Paul Krugman, "How Fast Can the US Economy Grow?" *Harvard Business Review*, July 1997, http://hbr.org/1997/07/how-fast-can-the-us-economy-grow/ar/1.

But, the potential lessons go deeper. The widespread belief in the 1980s and 1990s was that macroeconomic policy --which primarily uses fiscal and monetary policy to influence the demand side of the economy-- could do little to lower unemployment. That is because economists and policymakers believed that unemployment was primarily due to supply-side factors such as powerful unions, high minimum wages, generous unemployment insurance benefits, and other "labor-market rigidities". As a result, governments in the United States --and especially in Europe-- used macroeconomic policy sparingly or not at all in their efforts to increase employment. In Europe, macroeconomic policy, especially monetary policy connected with the creation of the single currency, arguably often worked actively against lowering unemployment.

The boom of the late 1990s was, instead, fueled by a stock-market bubble. As the boom got underway, the Federal Reserve Board made a decision not to counteract the expansionary effects of mounting stock-market wealth until there were clear signs that the increase in demand was causing the economy to overheat and leading inflation to rise. Despite the beliefs of most economists at the time, prices did not take off. In fact, inflation moved little, even by the time that the tech bubble burst in 2000-2001. Rising demand led to lower and lower unemployment --eventually hovering near 4.0 percent-- but without any significant rise inflation. This experiment proved that supply-side factors were not the cause of unemployment.

The problem with bubble-fueled growth was not that it produced inflation --it did not. Instead, the problem was that the resulting growth was not sustainable, and worse, it left the economy with a hangover that slowed employment growth in the subsequent recovery.[2] Seen in this light, the tech bubble of the late 1990s strongly supports the feasibility of --and the broad scope for-- expansionary macroeconomic policy.

When unemployment is high, economic policymakers would do well, at the very least, to follow the example of the Federal Reserve Board from the late 1990s: enact expansionary policies until there are signs that inflation is accelerating at an unacceptable rate. The tech boom inadvertently demonstrated that economic estimates of full employment were too conservative. Given the high social cost of unemployment, including the impact on inequality, a strong case exists for using macroeconomic policy to test empirically for the point where --in practice, not in theory-- the economy reaches full employment.

Expansionary monetary and fiscal policy are much better tools for reaching and maintaining full employment than the asset bubbles of the 1990s and 2000s. First, while there are real challenges, fine-tuning monetary and

---

[2] In many respects the 2001 recession and recovery were a dry-run for the much more severe recession of 2007-2009 with its even more sluggish recovery.

fiscal policy is much easier than trying to control asset bubbles. Second, policymakers have a much easier time combating a policy-induced acceleration in inflation (quick increases in interest rates, for example), than they do cleaning up after a burst asset bubble (as the current anemic recovery demonstrates with great clarity).

Conclusion

High unemployment is a social scourge, but the damage is not limited to those who lose their jobs. The needlessly high unemployment maintained during most of the last three decades has reduced the bargaining power of all workers, including those who manage to avoid being laid off. The experience of the late 1990s, when sustained low unemployment spurred broad and rapid wage growth for the only period in the last three decades, illustrates the central role that full employment should play in any plan to attack high and rising inequality.

.

17. Is There Really a Shortage of Skilled Workers?

Heidi Shierholz, Economist, Economic Policy Institute, Washington, DC

Skill shortage versus aggregate demand shortage as the cause of high unemployment

As of mid-summer 2013, more than four years since the start of the recovery from the Great Recession, the unemployment rate was 7.4 percent. This is far higher than the highest unemployment rate of the early 2000s downturn, 6.3 percent. Nevertheless, 7.4 percent is a substantial improvement from the high of 10.0 percent in October 2009. Is this reason to celebrate? Unfortunately, no. It turns out that most of the improvement has happened for all the wrong reasons, with the vast majority of the decline in the unemployment rate being due to workers dropping out of, or never entering, the labor force due to weak job opportunities (N.B. jobless workers are not counted as being unemployed and in the labor force unless they are actively seeking work).

The Congressional Budget Office estimates that if we were at full employment, the labor force would now number about 159.2 million, but the actual labor force is just 155.8 million. That means there are 3.4 million "missing workers" – jobless workers who would be in the labor force if job opportunities were stronger, but in the current environment are not actively seeking work and are therefore not counted. If those missing workers were in the labor force looking for work, the unemployment rate would be 9.4 percent instead of 7.4 percent. In other words, more than five-and-a-half years since the start of the Great Recession, the labor market remains extremely weak by historical standards.

One potential explanation for the extremely weak US jobs recovery is "skills mismatch," whereby workers do not have the skills for the jobs that are available. There is a sizeable literature on whether a skills mismatch is a driver of today's weak jobs recovery, and the strong consensus is that the weak labor market recovery is not due to skills mismatch (or any other structural factors). Instead, it is due to weakness in aggregate demand. For example, a 2012 paper by Edward Lazear (chief economist for George W. Bush) and James Spletzer states:

> "An analysis of labor market data suggests that there are no structural changes that can explain movements in unemployment rates over recent years. Neither industrial nor demographic shifts nor a mismatch of skills with job vacancies is behind the increased

rates of unemployment. ... The patterns observed are consistent with unemployment being caused by cyclic phenomena that are more pronounced during the current recession than in prior recessions." (Lazear et al, 2012)

Despite the clear consensus among researchers that the unambiguous problem is a shortfall of aggregate demand, there is a strong public narrative that today's jobs recovery is weak because workers don't have the right skills. Why? One reason may be psychological – it's easier to blame workers for lack of skills rather than face the fact that millions cannot find work no matter what they do because the jobs simply are not there. That in turn makes it easy for stories and anecdotes about employers who cannot find workers with the skills they need to circulate unscrutinized.

Another reason is political, since the cause of high unemployment is vitally important for policy. If high unemployment is due to workers not having the right skills, then the correct policy prescription is to focus on education and training, and macroeconomic policy to boost aggregate demand will not reduce unemployment. Policymakers and commentators who are against fiscal stimulus have a strong incentive to accept and propagate the myth that today's high unemployment is because workers lack the right skills.

The evidence

The key insight unpinning the evidence presented here is that if today's high unemployment were a problem of mismatches or a skills shortage, we would expect to find some types of workers or sectors or occupations of meaningful size now facing tight labor markets relative to before the recession started. The "signature" of skills mismatch is shortages relative to 2007 in some consequentially-sized groups of workers.

Figure 1 shows the unemployment rate by education, both in 2007 and over the last year (the 12-month period from August 2012-July 2013). It shows that workers with higher levels of education currently face – as they always do -- substantially lower unemployment rates than other workers. However, they too have seen large percentage increases in unemployment. Workers with a college degree or more still have unemployment rates that are more than one-and-a-half times as high as they were before the recession began. In other words, demand for workers at all levels of education is significantly weaker now than it was before the recession started. There is no evidence of workers at any level of education facing tight labor markets relative to 2007.

Figure 1: High unemployment at all levels of education relative to 2007

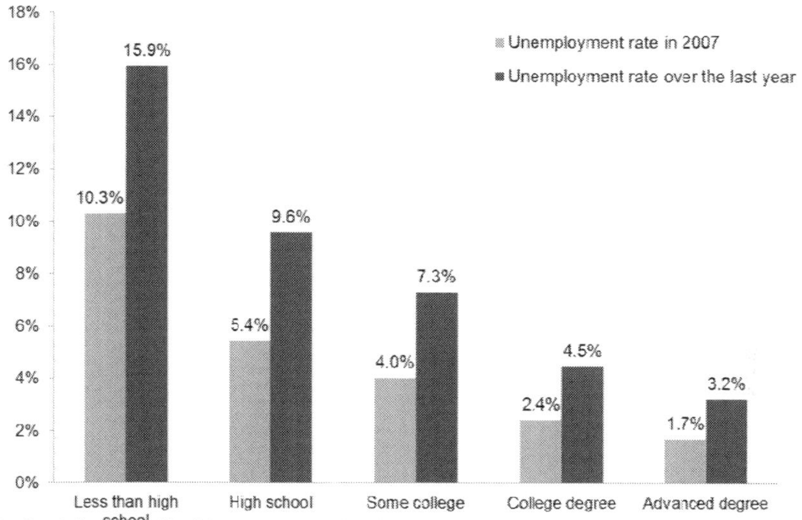

Note: Due to the fact that the data are not seasonally adjusted, 12 month averages are used. The last 12 months consist of data from August 2012 to July 2013.
Source: Author's analysis of Current Population Survey microdata

Figure 2 shows the unemployment rate by detailed occupation in 2007 and 2012. As is always the case, some occupations in 2012 have higher unemployment rates than others. However, the unemployment rate in 2012 in all occupations is higher than it was before the recession. In every occupational category demand for workers is lower than it was five years ago. The signature of a skills mismatch – workers in some occupations experiencing tight labor markets relative to 2007 – is plainly missing.

Another valuable source for diagnosing the cause of the current sustained high unemployment is the data on job openings. Figure 3 shows the number of unemployed workers and the number of job openings by industry. Again, if high elevated unemployment were due to skills shortages or mismatches, we would expect to find some sectors where there are more unemployed workers than job openings, and some sectors where there are more job openings than unemployed workers. However, unemployed workers dramatically outnumber job openings in all sectors. There are between 1.4 and 10.5 times as many unemployed workers as job openings in every industry. Even in the industry (Finance and Insurance) with the most favorable ratio of unemployed workers to job openings, there are still 40 percent more unemployed workers than job openings. In no industry does the number of job openings even come close to the number of people looking for work.

Figure 2: High unemployment in all occupations relative to 2007

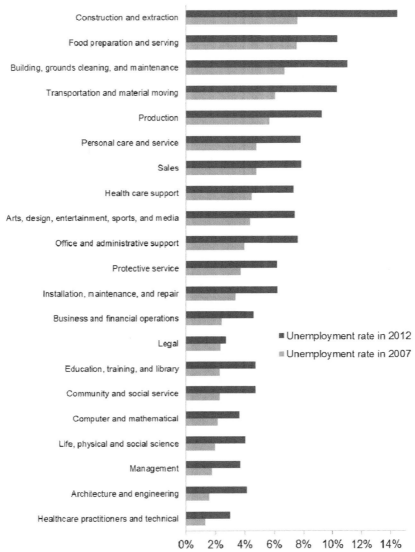

Source: Authors' analysis of basic monthly Current Population Survey microdata

Furthermore, a job opening when the labor market is weak often does not mean the same thing as a job opening when the labor market is strong. There is a wide range of "recruitment intensity" with which a company can deal with a job opening. For example, if a company is trying hard to fill an opening, it may increase the compensation package and/or scale back the required qualifications. Conversely, if it is not trying very hard, it may hike up the required qualifications and/or offer a meager compensation package. Perhaps unsurprisingly, research shows that recruitment intensity is cyclical: it tends to be stronger when the labor market is strong, and weaker when the labor market is weak (Davis, et al, 2012). This means that when a job opening goes unfilled when the labor market is weak, as it is today, companies may very well be holding out for an overly qualified candidate at a very cheap price. .

Figure 3. Unemployed vatly outnumber job openings across the board
Unemployed and job openings, by industry (in thousands)

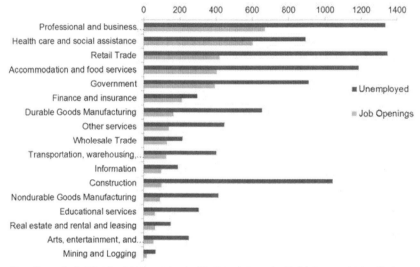

Note: Due to the fact that the data are not seasonally adjusted, these are 12-month averages, July 2012– June 2013.

Another way to approach the question of whether or not the labor market is suffering from skills mismatch is to note that if employers really did have enough demand for their goods and services to need to hire new people but couldn't find suitable workers, they would be ramping up the hours of the workers they have. Figure 4 shows average weekly hours in 2012 as a percentage of average weekly hours in 2007 by occupation. Only in legal occupations are hours meaningfully longer than they were before the recession began, though the average workweek in legal occupations increased by less than one percent in those five years. Given that in almost all occupations the average weekly hours of existing workers are lower now than they were before the recession started, it is difficult to see how employers are seeing demand go unmet because they can't find people who can do the work.

Figure 4: No evidence of hours being ramped up
Weekly hours in 2012 relative to 2007, by occupation

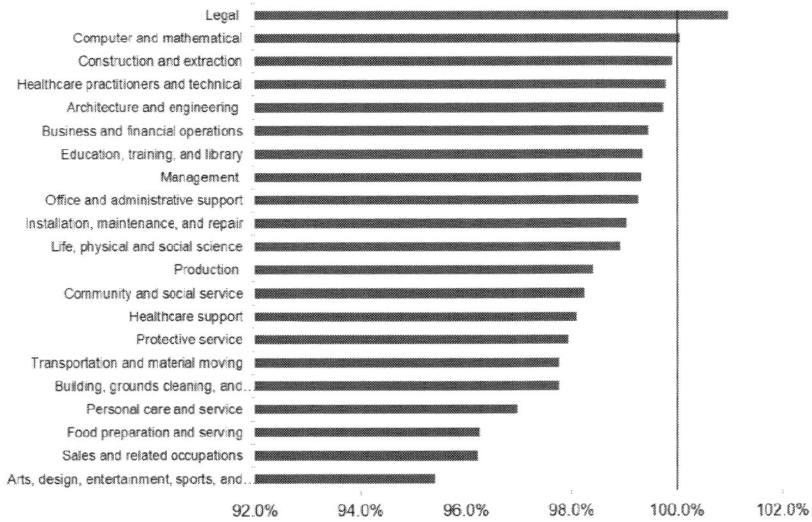

Source: Author's analysis of basic monthly Current Population Survey microdata

Another place to look for evidence of a skills shortage is in wage trends. If skills are in short supply, the simple logic of supply and demand implies wages should be increasing substantially in occupations where there is a shortage of skilled labor. In other words, employers who face shortages of suitable, interested workers should be responding by bidding up wages to attract the workers they need. Figure 5 shows average hourly wages in 2012 as a percentage of average hourly wages in 2007 by occupation, along with productivity growth over this same period as a benchmark for the rate at which average wages should grow. In no occupation is there any hint of wages being bid up in a way that would indicate tight labor markets or labor shortages. In fact, in no occupation have average wages even kept pace with overall productivity growth over this period. This pattern of productivity growth outstripping wage growth across the board is a signature of weak demand for workers caused by shortage of demand for goods and services, not skills mismatch.

In sum, no matter how you cut the data, there is no evidence of skills shortages as a major cause of today's elevated unemployment. The evidence on wages, hours, job openings, and unemployment across demographic groups, industries, and occupations, all confirm broad-based weakened demand for workers.

Figure 5: No evidence of wages being bid up
Real average hourly wages in 2012 relative to 2007, by occupation

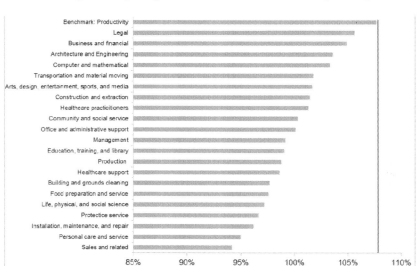

Source: Author's analysis of Bureau of Labor Statistics' Current Population Survey

Other possible causes of high unemployment

What about other structural shifts aside from skills mismatches? One to consider is "housing lock" whereby problems in the housing market may mean individuals are locked into communities in which jobs are scarce. However, like the skills mismatch myth, housing lock has been rigorously investigated and rejected as a key driver of today's persistent high unemployment (Farber, 2012; Lazear, et al, 2012; Rothstein, 2012).

Another argument is that today's high unemployment is due to the unemployment insurance (UI) extensions in the Great Recession and its aftermath. However, this too has been rigorously investigated and UI extensions have been found to have had at most a very modest impact on the amount of time people remain unemployed. Moreover, the small increase in unemployment duration due to UI extensions is primarily due to the fact that unemployed workers who receive UI are less likely to give up looking for work, because an active job search is a requirement for receiving benefits. This is a positive feature since keeping workers attached to the labor market may increase the likelihood they will eventually find work rather than entering the pool of hidden unemployment made up of discouraged workers. Of course, the effects of extended UI benefits are likely to disappear when those benefits expire, as they have already begun to do (Daly, et al, 2012; Farber, et al, 2013; Rothstein, 2012).

Conclusion: it's aggregate demand, stupid!

There are simply no structural changes capable of explaining the pattern of sustained high unemployment over the last five years. What we have, instead, is an aggregate demand problem. The reason we are not seeing robust job growth is because businesses have not seen demand for their goods and services pick up in a way that would require them to significantly ramp up hiring. The right policies for the present moment are, therefore, straightforward. More education and training to help workers make job transitions could help some individuals, but it's not going to generate demand, so it will not solve the unemployment crisis. Instead, Washington policymakers must to focus on policies that will stimulate demand. In the current moment this can only be reliably accomplished through expansionary fiscal policy involving such measures as large-scale ongoing public investments and the reestablishment of state and local public services that were cut in the Great Recession and its aftermath.

References

Daly, Mary C., Bart Hobijn, Aysegul Sahin, and Robert G. Valletta (2012), "A search and matching approach to labor markets: Did the natural rate of unemployment rise?" *Journal of Economic Perspectives*, Volume 26, Number 3, pp. 3-26.

Davis, Steven J., R. Jason Faberman, and John C. Haltiwanger (2012), "The establishment-level behavior of vacancies and hiring", National Bureau of Economic Research Working Paper No. 16265.

Farber, Henry S. (2012), "Unemployment in the Great Recession: Did the housing market crisis prevent the unemployed from moving to take jobs?" *American Economic Review Papers and Proceedings*, 102(2), pp. 520-525.

Farber, Henry S. and Robert G. Valletta (2013), "Do extended unemployment benefits lengthen unemployment spells? Evidence from recent cycles in the US labor market," Federal Reserve Bank of San Francisco Working Paper No. 2013-09.

Lazear, Edward P. and James R. Spletzer (2012), "The United States labor market: Status quo or a new normal?" National Bureau of Economic Research Working Paper No. 18386.

Rothstein, Jesse (2012), "The labor market four years into the crisis: Assessing structural explanations", National Bureau of Economic Research Working Paper No. 17966.

18. Institutions to Remedy the New Inequality

William E. Spriggs, *Chief Economist, AFL-CIO, Washington, DC,* *wspriggs@aflcio.org.*

The challenge of technology

The current era congratulates itself for being the age of innovation. Computers, and the technologies they have made possible in communications, have reduced the cost of management of far-flung enterprises and sped the flow of information and content to the speed of light. However, this fundamental change and the rapid deployment of technology, has also created an equally rapid restructuring of work and wages, creating massive inequality between those riding the crest of the new technology and those being replaced by it.

A tale of two technological revolutions.

But, this age is not so revolutionary. Engage for a moment in a thought experiment. Imagine you are a young lieutenant in the US Cavalry on your horse on the outskirts of Petersburg, Virginia in the waning days of the US Civil War. You are in the midst of trench warfare, and it is March 1865. Your assignments include efforts to attack telegraph lines and railroads. Now, imagine in the midst of the smoke of war, you are transported Twilight Zone style to the Meuse-Argonne offensive of the Western Front in World War I, where the objective of the 2nd US Calvary was severing the German supply lines of the Sedan-Merieres railroad. It is October 1918.

What a world of difference the young lieutenant would confront. No cavalry charges because the increased capabilities of warfare have made them obsolete. The young lieutenant who witnessed the beginnings of trench warfare in Petersburg would probably understand that change in tactic. But, the rest of the world, less than fifty years in time, would be bizarre. He would see airplanes flying overhead patrolling the skies and engaging in combat, able to strafe forces on the ground or drop bombs on them. He would see officers on the ground talking into a "radio" to communicate with the pilots in the air, and would learn that the pilots were able to talk to each other using "radios" while their planes were yards apart up in the air. Crude tanks would roam the battlefield, and if he wasn't careful he would be run over by fast moving automobiles; advances in transportation that would make someone only accustomed to trains marvel.

If he returned to the officer's barracks, he would have been confronted with strange electric lights, or startled when they would play music on a phonograph and listen to Al Jolson's "Rock-A-Bye Your Baby With a Dixie Melody," or perhaps the Original Dixieland Jazz Band playing "Tiger Rag." A trip to Paris would have included a visit to a motion picture, perhaps D.W. Griffith's "Hearts of the World" or Charlie Chaplin's "Shoulder Arms." These are forms of entertainment our Civil War hero could only vaguely have imagined within his 1865 reference frame based on still photography and music boxes. His Paris host may have phoned to invite a friend to join them for dinner. The telephone may have been his smallest shock since he was familiar with the telegraph, but he might have been amused when the telephone was used to call another person in the same city for personal communication.

The new world our lieutenant would enter shows the scale of transformation that took place in less than fifty years. New industries were launched in telephones and personal communications, automobiles, air craft and airlines, motion pictures, phonographs, electric light bulbs, radio and the electrification of manufacturing. His world, dominated by machine innovations like sewing machines, agricultural implements, textiles and railroad engines and rail cars would make some of this comprehensible. However, these new industries were coupled with changes in the size of manufacturers and industrial organization. Products that had been dominated by local production were replaced with national brands and factories that could meet national demand.

He would have missed the advent of advertising and the rise of advertising as a means to undergird publications that would further the spread of information at lower costs. In 1882, Proctor and Gamble launched a $266,000 (in 2013 dollars, author's calculation based on Federal Reserve bank of Minneapolis, 2013) campaign for Ivory Soap when Americans learned it was "99 and 44/100% pure". By 1898 NABISCO would be launching a million dollar campaign for the nationally marketed pre-packaged "Uneeda" biscuit, and in 1912 Morton would advance its tagline "When it Rains, It Pours." (Advertising Age, 1999)

We marvel today at the rate of adaptation of our technology, scoffing at the snail's pace spread of the telephone. But, it is crucial to understand that these new inventions were so novel, the adaptation we see as natural was slow to occur at the time. The initial impulse behind the telephone was seen as a competitor to the telegraph. Initially telephone lines were not a network, but a wire run for point-to-point communication on a private line. In part this was a technological issue, switching equipment needed to be created, but in larger part it was a vision issue; locked into a world of public infrastructures, finance and institutions that were slow to adapt to totally new ways of thinking and doing things. The spread of the telephone should not be measured from its patent in 1876, but to the understanding of its potential as a personal communication device (Carre, 1993). Similarly for the "wireless telegraph," the radio and its diffusion cannot be dated to its patent in 1896. Again, it was initially seen as a way to get around the monopolies of the telegraph companies and the limitations of wires to reach vessels at sea, and it took some time to see the possibilities and value of broadcasting a radio signal.

These issues are raised because the era our brave Civil War hero time-travelled to was populated with ideas and conventions that were totally unforeseen. These ideas brought change that was not just a matter of improvements in speed or efficiency: they brought changes in world outlook.

Now, imagine a similar experiment. This time imagine the young lieutenant is swept off to Vietnam in 1964 with the 1st US Cavalry. He is among troops waiting for helicopters to arrive from the USS Boxer, an American aircraft carrier that is miles away and out of sight in the Gulf of Tonkin. This cavalry has no horses—the helicopters are their horses. He will soon learn that his comrades will call for air support from Anderson Air Force Base in Guam, an island over 2,450 miles east in the Pacific Ocean. The troops will relax to music played on radios and when they get to Saigon, they may get a chance to watch television or see a movie. Having travelled through time, almost another fifty years, he will be impressed that aircraft are much superior to the ones he saw in World War I France. He knew of radio to communicate to airplanes from World War I, and so would be amused that now radios would be used to broadcast music. Television would be an interesting extension of the movies he saw, and he would be impressed that the movies now had color and sound. He already understood from World War I that as combat evolved horses would not be part of a future army. And, he would also be impressed that the modern Jeep was much better than the automobiles he saw in World War I. It would take longer to explain that satellites in space made it possible to get television signals from home. The ideas of rockets and space travel and men-in-space are a stretch from the crude airplanes he saw in France in 1918, but logically plausible looking at the jet bombers from Anderson Air Base. But, none of these would be new concepts. They would be extreme improvements on a path of technological improvements he might have extrapolated from based on what he saw in changes from 1865 to 1918.

Perhaps, he would have been more shocked at the bigger change in society and the description of the lives of the soldiers he encountered. Several of the troops would have been to college, and most would have finished high school. The home lives they would describe, living in houses with radios and televisions, riding buses to school; they would appear to be wealthy, highly educated troops compared to what he knew in 1865 or 1918. And, while he fought at Petersburg alongside the largest gathering of African

American troops of the Civil War, he would be surprised that African Americans were officers commanding white troops and integrated into the force -- especially seeing how African American troops had been treated in France in 1918, segregated away from American troops and forced to fight alongside the French. The technologies would be very impressive, but the change in American society would have looked unimaginable.

Now, let our brave lieutenant jump in time again, this time to somewhere in Zabul province of Afghanistan with the 1st US Calvary in May 2013. Much faster and lighter helicopters whisk him with his new comrades out to the field. They will, as in Vietnam, use their radios to communicate with air support. He will notice the radios are much smaller and lighter. He will also see that the air support is able to get much closer to their position, because the troops have devices showing their exact location. The troops in Vietnam had explained to him there were now satellites in space that could communicate back and forth to earth over great distances. His new comrades explain how the system of satellites lets them get their precise location to share with artillery and air support. When he goes back to base, he sees the soldiers are able to send messages home using what looks like the typewriters he saw in World War I and looking at screens that resemble the television sets he saw in Vietnam. Using their "computers", they can see family members they are talking to back home. The accuracy and precision of everything is quite surprising to him, and the speed of everything is a long way from what he saw in Vietnam. But, again, the concepts are logical progressions from World War I in 1918 and Vietnam in 1964.

With machines that were faster and more complex than those he saw in 1964, he would be struck that little was changed regarding the soldiers. They were not greatly more educated than those he saw in 1964. Their family and home lives didn't seem very different from the Vietnam soldiers; not like the gap between the Vietnam soldiers and those of World War I or World War I soldiers and his Civil War comrades.

Institutional failure or technology as the cause of rising income inequality?

Hopefully, this thought experiment suggests that while ordinary lives improved slowly from the technology innovations that took place between 1865 and 1918 and that truly ushered in the modern-era, it was the institutional changes from 1918 to 1964 that created a broad based middle-class lifestyle of the troops that made the movement through time shocking. And, while we marvel at our current computer-era advances, they pale relative to the creation of radio, electric lights, airplanes, automobiles, telephones, motion pictures and sound recordings; innovations that were truly discontinuous shifts in human progress. Most importantly, we have yet to make the institutional changes needed to ensure our own era of technological advances continues and advances a broad based middle-class lifestyle.

There is a large body of research on wages in response to the rapid innovation of the late nineteenth and early twentieth century. The dominant story is that the modern era ushered in a rise in wage inequality that began to shrink near the Great Depression (Lindert & Williamson, 1980). Revisionists to that story are now using new data to argue a more nuanced telling of the 1865 to 1929 period. One argument is that there was a "hollowing" out of the income distribution. The argument is that the telegraph, typewriter and electric lights led to a more productive white collar skilled work force, while electrification and mass production hollowed out the skills of craftsmen replacing them with production workers at the lower end (Gray, 2013). This characterization follows an argument that the expansion of manufacturing in the US replaced skill workers, and was a complement to unskilled workers (James & Skinner, 1985).

Little is offered of institutional factors in contributing to wage movements of the period. Skilled workers were often unionized, relying on their monopoly of the skills. Manufacturing workers were in unions without the protection of labor laws that recognized unions or the right to organize. However, changes in labor market institutions are well understood to explain a substantial portion of the rapid wage compression that occurred in the 1940s (Goldin & Margo, 1992). The power of those institutions kept wages together until the 1970s.

What the data shows is that inequality began to rise as those institutions began to unravel, and it also shows the importance of the industries where those institutions worked best. Because the long climb to present levels of inequality pre-dates the rise of the computer age, it would be more accurate to discuss the current situation as exacerbating the declining influence of workplace institutions of the Depression era.

Updating today's labor market institutions to meet the challenge of technology.

What is missing today is discussion of the type of institutions that fit the new post-manufacturing era so that the benefits of mass technological change can be harnessed to create a new broad and inclusive middle class? Models of unions predicated on bargaining units defined to reflect organizing workers in a single large facility do not fit the current world of smaller factories and far flung employees. The evolution of new work arrangements distances workers from the source of the value-added; a janitor may work for a company that is a subcontractor to maintenance firm that is a subcontractor to a parts company that is a subcontractor to the final product. Each layer of distance makes it more difficult to connect workers to their value-added in the chain, and makes efforts at organizing more tenuous. Consequently, the old model of a union representing a set of workers for the same employer is a poor fit.

A new set of labor laws is required that allows workers to organize and represent their voice in decision making across place and through contracting layers. The protection of employers from secondary boycotts granted by the Taft-Hartley amendments to the National Labor Relations Act is no longer founded in a world where secondary boycotts are too great a weapon for labor.

Meanwhile, nothing has shown the minimum wage to be more important than the post 1980 era when the value of the minimum wage was allowed to lose its relationship to productivity and the average wage. The bottom is losing out because we have lowered the bottom. This is a perverted way to maintain "skill-wage" gaps. It makes the gap of those at the top one percent grow compared to the middle, while consoling the middle that they remain ahead of the bottom. That is not so different from the plantation masters who let poor whites feel superior because of the inferior treatment to African Americans.

A non-labor institution that was important in leveling the wage distribution after 1929 was the early twentieth century expansion of high school education. The "public high school" movement of the late nineteenth century took hold, and the rapid increase in high school educated workers helped lower the education premium. No similar movement is afoot today. Instead, as the 21st Century has dawned, America has lowered its investment in higher education by raising the cost of college for students. Despite this, college graduation rates have been increasing, but at a tremendous cost to the middle class that is not sustainable. Oddly, in all the screams about tuition, there has not been the same screaming about the cut in investment in colleges. And, the solutions being offered are not the massive investment made in the early 20th century to build and support free public high schools with a commitment to free university education.

Another non-labor institution is a recommitment to equality. New barriers, whether to immigration status or to ex-felon status is creating a huge surplus of workers with limited rights and mobility that face limited job prospects. These barriers must be removed to make a path to an inclusive and broad based middle class possible.

While there is little vision for an economic policy to get us out of the rut we are in, there is even less vision of a new order for the middle class. In 1930, the Great Depression caused a serious examination of how the labor market failed to produce the right outcomes of rising wages and living standards that match advances in technology and human possibility. Today, there is no great examination of the market. Instead, we have settled that the market is working as expected, grinding many into poverty and reducing the middle class to the poor. There is no sense that the market needs new rules and limits.

The correct answer is not that the market has made the billionaires of this era, as the previous century made its millionaires, and we must accept this condition. That was not answer before, and it is not the answer today. In fact, our current system led us to the brink of economic collapse, and it may yet produce political turmoil resulting in despots and evil on a global scale. The implication is we must tame the market or be doomed to despots and evil.

Doing so requires creating a new language and way of explaining where we are, and why we are in this position. Markets are not absolute. Markets are simply mechanisms that work within a framework. At the moment, that framework protects a few people, who obviously want to defend this framework. But, a better framework can be designed that rewards those who work hard and protects those failed by the market. In the past the market rewarded hard work and it is the fear of too many that changing the rules will take away their benefits. But as the rules have been changed, the current market benefits those who can skim output from the top and who can outsource the jobs—not the job creators, but the job robbers.

The first members of the United Auto Workers believed they were autonomous, using their combined voices to affect their fate. Today, new institutions are needed that reassure people of their fundamental belief in their autonomy to control their fate, and these new institutions must also give workers new tools to take the power to make that possible.

References

Advertising Age (1999), Ad Age Advertising Century: Timeline. Advertising Age, March.

Carre, P. (1993), Uncertain Development - Diffusion of the Telephone in France before 1914. Réseaux. *The French journal of communication*, 1 (2), 245-260.

Federal Reserve Bank of Minneapolis (2013), Community and Education. Retrieved September 16, 2013, from MinneapolisFed.org: http://www.minneapolisfed.org/community_education/teacher/calc/hist1800.cfm

Goldin, C., & Margo, R. A. (1992), The Great Compression: The Wage Structure in the United States at Mid-Century. *The Quarterly Journal of Economics*, 107 (1), 1-34.

Gray, R. (2013), Taking Technology to Task: The skill content in technological change in early Twentieth Century United States. *Explorations in Economic History*, 50 (3), 351-367.

James, J., & Skinner, J. (1985), The Resolution of the Labor-Scarcity Paradox. *Journal of Economic History*, 45 (3), 513-540.

Lindert, P., & Williamson, J. (1980), *American Inequality: A Macroeconomic History*. New York: Academic Press.

V
Refashioning Capitalism To Deliver Shared Prosperity

19. Finance-Dominated Capitalism and Income Distribution: Implications for Shared Prosperity

Eckhard Hein, *P.h.D, Professor, Berlin School of Economics and Law, Badensche Str. 50-51, 10825 Berlin, Germany. eckhard.hein@hwr-berlin.de*

Introduction

It is now widely agreed that the severity of the financial and economic crises in the period 2007-2012 is attributable to a combination of worsened income distribution over the last decades, large current account imbalances at the global and regional (euro area) levels, and malfunctioning deregulated financial markets.[1] These outcomes are associated with the era of 'financialization' or 'finance-dominated capitalism',[2] a long-run development which has dominated the US and the UK since the late 1970s/early 1980s and spread to other developed capitalist economies in the course of the 1980s and 1990s.

Financialization is associated with several adverse features. A first major feature has been the re-distribution of income at the expense of (low) labour incomes and in favour of gross profits (retained earnings, dividends, interest) as well as top management salaries.

A second feature of financialization has been the depressing effect on investment in capital stock, caused by increasing shareholder value orientation of management. On the one hand this has meant increasing short-termism regarding profitability favouring highly profitable short-term financial investment instead of long-term real investment in the firm. On the other, hand it has meant the drain of internal means of finance potentially available for real investment purposes from the corporations, through increasing dividend payments and share buybacks in order to boost stock prices and thus shareholder value.

A third major feature of financialization has been an increasing potential for wealth-based and debt-financed consumption. In several countries, stock market and housing price booms each increased notional wealth against which households were willing to borrow. Changing financial norms, new financial instruments (credit card debt, home equity lending), deterioration of creditworthiness standards, triggered by securitisation of mortgage debt and

---

[1] See, for example, UNCTAD (2012), Stiglitz (2012), Palley (2012; 2013) and Hein (2012).
[2] On the macroeconomics of finance-dominated capitalism see Hein (2012) and the empirical and theoretical literature referred to in that book.

'originate and distribute' strategies of banks, made increasing credit available to low income, low wealth households, in particular. This allowed for consumption to rise faster than median income and thus to stabilise aggregate demand. But it also generated increasing debt-income ratios of private households and thus increasing financial fragility for the economy as a whole.

A fourth feature of financialization has been the deregulation and liberalisation of international capital markets and the capital accounts, which has created the potential to run and to finance persistent current account deficits. Simultaneously it also created the problems of foreign indebtedness, speculative capital movements, exchange rate volatilities and related currency crises.

Against the background of these basic macroeconomic tendencies of finance-dominated capitalism, rising current account imbalances at the global, but also at the European level, developed and contributed to the severity of the Great Recession 2008/09, and in Europe to the following euro crisis. Countries like the US, the UK and Spain, for example, relied on debt-led soaring private consumption demand as the main driver of aggregate demand and GDP growth, generating and accepting concomitant rising deficits in their trade and current account balances. Other countries like Germany, Austria and the Netherlands, for example, focussed on mercantilist export-led strategies as an alternative to generating demand, in the face of redistribution at the expense of (low) labour incomes, stagnating consumption demand and weak real investment, and hence accumulated increasing surpluses in their trade and current account balances.[3] The financial crisis, which was triggered by over-indebtedness problems of private households in the leading 'debt-led consumption boom' economy, the US, could thus quickly spread to the 'export-led mercantilist' economies through the foreign trade channel (collapse of exports) and the financial contagion channel (devaluation of financial assets) and thus cause the world-wide Great Recession.

From this analysis it follows that any sustainable post-crisis growth model can neither rely on the 'debt-led consumption boom' nor on the 'export-led mercantilist' models of the past. Aggregate demand and growth rather have to be mass income or wage-led. Tackling the distribution problem is thus fundamental for any agenda of shared prosperity. Therefore, in the following section I will address the re-distribution processes during the pre-crisis financialization period and the most likely causes for falling labour income shares in particular. After that I will present the economic policy implications for an agenda of shared prosperity.

---

[3] See Hein (2012, Chapter 6) and Hein and Mundt (2012) for an extensive analysis of 'debt-led consumption boom' and 'mercantilist export-led' types of development based on a broad set of countries.

Table 1. Labour income share as percentage of GDP at current factor costs, average values over the trade cycle, early 1980s – 2008			
	1. Early 1980s – early 1990s	2. Early 1990s – early 2000s	3. Early 2000s – 2008	Change (3. – 1.), percentage points
Austria	75.66	70.74	65.20	-10.46
Belgium	70.63	70.74	69.16	-1.47
France	71.44	66.88	65.91	-5.53
Germany	67.11	66.04	63.34	-3.77
Greecea)	67.26	62.00	60.60	-6.66
Ireland	70.34	60.90	55.72	-14.61
Italy	68.31	63.25	62.37	-5.95
Netherlands	68.74	67.21	65.57	-3.17
Portugal	65.73	70.60	71.10	5.37
Spain	68.32	66.13	62.41	-5.91
Sweden	71.65	67.04	69.16	-2.48
UK	72.79	71.99	70.67	-2.12
US	68.20	67.12	65.79	-2.41
Japana)	72.38	70.47	65.75	-6.64

Notes: The labour income share is given by the compensation per employee divided by GDP at factor costs per person employed. The beginning of a trade cycle is given by a local minimum of annual real GDP growth in the respective country.
a) adjusted to fit in 3 cycle pattern
Data: European Commission (2010), author's calculations
Source: Hein (2012, p. 13)

Trends and causes of re-distribution since the early 1980s[4]

The period of finance-dominated capitalism has been associated with a massive redistribution of income. First, functional income distribution has changed at the expense of labour and in favour of broad capital income. The labour income share, as a measure taken from the national accounts and corrected for the changes in the composition of employment regarding employees and self-employed, shows a falling trend in the developed capitalist economies considered here from the early 1980s until the Great Recession. This is shown in Table 1, which presents cyclical averages in order to eliminate cyclical fluctuations due to the well-known counter-cyclical properties of the labour income share

---

[4] This section draws on Hein (2013).

Table 2. Gini coefficient before taxes for households' market income

Country	mid-80s	around 1990	mid-90s	around 2000	mid-2000s	late 2000s	Change from mid-80s/around 1990/mid 90s until late 2000s
Austria	..	..	..	..	0.433	0.472	..
Belgium	0.449	..	0.472	0.464	0.494	0.469	0.020
Finland	0.387	..	0.479	0.478	0.483	0.465	0.078
France	..	..	0.473	0.490	0.485	0.483	0.010
Germany	0.439	0.429	0.459	0.471	0.499	0.504	0.065
Greece	0.426	..	0.446	0.466	0.454	0.436	0.010
Ireland	..	..	..	..	..	..	..
Italy	0.420	0.437	0.508	0.516	0.557	0.534	0.114
Netherlands	0.473	0.474	0.484	0.424	0.426	0.426	-0.047
Portugal	..	0.436	0.490	0.479	0.542	0.521	0.085
Spain	..	..	..	..	..	0.461	..
Sweden	0.404	0.408	0.438	0.446	0.432	0.426	0.022
UK	0.419	0.439	0.453	0.512	0.500	0.506	0.087
US	0.436	0.450	0.477	0.476	0.486	0.486	0.050
Japan	0.345	..	0.403	0.432	0.443	0.462	0.117

Gini coefficient after taxes for households' disposable income

Country	mid-80s	around 1990	mid-90s	around 2000	mid-2000s	late 2000s	Change mid-80s/around 1990 until late 2000s
Austria	0.236	..	0.238	0.252	0.265	0.261	0.025
Belgium	0.274	..	0.287	0.289	0.271	0.259	-0.015
Finland	0.209	..	0.218	0.247	0.254	0.259	0.050
France	0.300	0.290	0.277	0.287	0.288	0.293	-0.007
Germany	0.251	0.256	0.266	0.264	0.285	0.295	0.044
Greece	0.336	..	0.336	0.345	0.321	0.307	-0.029
Ireland	0.331	..	0.324	0.304	0.314	0.293	-0.038
Italy	0.309	0.297	0.348	0.343	0.352	0.337	0.028
Netherlands	0.272	0.292	0.297	0.292	0.284	0.294	0.022
Portugal	..	0.329	0.359	0.356	0.385	0.353	0.024
Spain	0.371	0.337	0.343	0.342	0.319	0.317	-0.054
Sweden	0.198	0.209	0.211	0.243	0.234	0.259	0.061
UK	0.309	0.354	0.336	0.352	0.331	0.342	0.033
US	0.337	0.348	0.361	0.357	0.38	0.378	0.041
Japan	0.304	..	0.323	0.337	0.321	0.329	0.025

Note: Gini coefficient is based on equivalised household income
Data: OECD (2012), author's calculations
Source: Hein (2013, p. 7)

Second, personal income distribution has become more unequal in most of the countries from the mid 1980s until the late 2000s. Taking the Gini coefficient as an indicator, this is true for the distribution of market income, with the Netherlands being the only exception in the data set (Table 2). If re-distribution via taxes and social policies by the state is included and the distribution of disposable income is considered, Belgium, France, Greece, Ireland, and Spain have not seen an increase in their Gini coefficients. The other countries, however, have also experienced increasing inequality in distribution of disposable income in the period of finance-dominated capitalism.

Third, as data based on tax reports provided by Alvaredo et al. (2012) have shown, there has been an explosion of the shares of the very top incomes since the early 1980s in the US and the UK, which prior to the present crisis have again reached levels of the mid-1920s in the US and the mid-1930s in the UK (Figure 1). Although Germany has not yet seen such an increase, it should be noted that the share of the top 0.1 per cent has been substantially higher in this country longer periods of time and that it has only been surpassed by the US and the UK in the mid 1980s and the mid-1990s, respectively (Figure 2).

Figure 1. Top 0.1 per cent share in national income in the UK and the US, in per cent

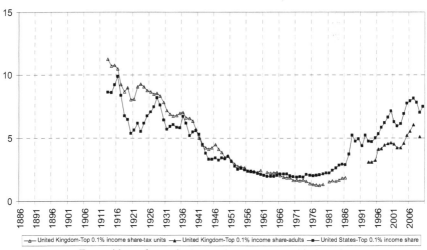

Data: Alvaredo et al. (2012). Source: Hein (2013, p. 9

Figure 2. Top 0.1 per cent share in national income in Germany, in per cent

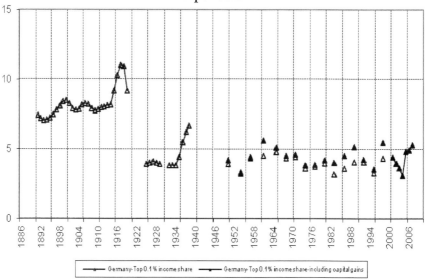

Data: Alvaredo et al. (2012).

Figure 3. Composition of top 0.1 per cent income, US, 1950-2010

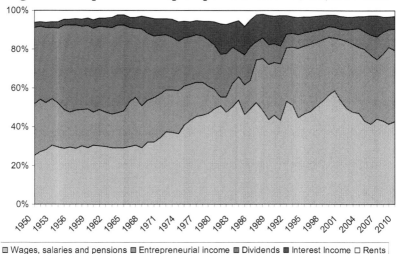

Data: Alvaredo et al. (2012). Source: Hein (2013, p. 12).

Taking a look at the composition of top incomes, the increase in the income share of the top 0.1 per cent in the US has mainly been driven by an increase in top salaries (wages and salaries, bonuses, exercised stock-options and pensions) since the 1970s, and since the mid 1980s also in entrepreneurial income (Figure 3). Remuneration of top management ('working rich') has therefore contributed significantly, but not exclusively, to rising inequality in the US from the early 1980s until 2006. Whereas top management salaries have contributed up to more than 50 per cent to the income of the top 0.1 per cent income share in the US, in Germany top management salaries have played a minor role. However, their share increased from 15 per cent in 1992 to 22.4 per cent in 2003 (Bach et al., 2009). Therefore, the 'working rich' phenomenon seems to arise in Germany as well.

Since top management salaries are part of compensation of employees in the national accounts and are thus included in the labour income share considered above, the increase in top management salaries has dampened the fall in the measured labour income share since the early 1980s. Excluding top management salaries from the labour income share would therefore give an even more pronounced fall in the share of 'direct labour', as has been shown by Buchele and Christiansen (2007) and Glyn (2009) for the US and by Dünhaupt (2011) for Germany and the US.

According to Atkinson (2009), the trends and determinants of functional income distribution provide the key to the explanation of the other dimensions of redistribution. The analysis of factor shares provides the link between incomes at the macroeconomic or the national accounting level and incomes at the level of the household, thus helping to understand the development of inequality in personal distribution, and providing an indicator of the relative powers of different groups. In Hein (2013), I have therefore reviewed the recent empirical literature on the determinants of income shares against the background of the Kaleckian theory of distribution, in order to identify the channels through which financialization and neo-liberalism have affected functional income distribution (Table 3).[5]

According to the Kaleckian approach (Kalecki 1954, Part I), the gross profit share in national income, which includes retained earnings, dividend, interest and rent payments, as well as overhead costs (thus also top management salaries) has three major determinants.

First, the profit share is affected by firms' pricing in incompletely competitive goods markets, i.e. by the mark-up on unit variable costs. The mark-up itself is determined by the degree of industrial concentration and by the relevance of price competition relative to other instruments of competition (marketing, product differentiation) in the respective industries or sectors, i.e. by the degree of price competition in the goods market; by the bargaining power of trade unions, because in a heterogeneous environment with differences in unit wage cost growth between firms, industries or sectors,

---

[5] Neoliberalism is a broader concept than financialization, aiming at the deregulation of labour, financial and goods markets, reduction of government intervention into the market economy and of government demand management, and at re-distribution of income from wages to profits.

the firm's or the industry's ability to shift changes in nominal wage costs to prices is constrained by competition of other firms or industries which do not have to face the same increase in unit wage costs; and by overhead costs and gross profit targets, because the mark-up has to cover overhead costs and distributed profits.

**Table 3: Financialization and the gross profit share -
a Kaleckian perspective**

	Determinants of the gross profit share (including (top) management salaries)				
	1) Mark-up			2) Price of imported raw materials and semi-finished products	3) Sectoral composition of the domestic economy
Stylized facts of financialization (1.-7.) and neo-liberalism (8.-9.)	1.a) Degree of price competition in the goods market	1.b) Bargaining power and activity of trade union	1.c) Overhead costs and gross profit targets		
1. Increasing shareholder value orientation and short-termism of management	...	+	+	...	...
2. Rising dividend payments	...	...	+	...	...
3. Increasing interest rates or interest payments	...	...	+	...	...
4. Increasing top management salaries	...	...	+	...	...
5. Increasing relevance of financial to non-financial sector (investment)	...	+	...	...	+
6. Mergers and acquisitions	+	...	...	...	...
7. Liberalisation and globalisation of international finance and trade	−	+	...	+/−	+/−
8. Deregulation of the labour market	...	+	...	...	...
9. Downsizing of government	...	+	...	...	+

Notes: + positive effect on the gross profit share, − negative effect on the gross profit share, ... no direct effect on the gross profit share

Source: Hein (2013, p. 15).

Second, with mark-up pricing on unit variable costs, i.e. material plus wage costs, the profit share in national income is affected by unit imported material costs relative to unit wage costs. With a constant mark-up an increase in unit material costs will thus increase the profit share in national income.

And third, the aggregate profit share of the economy as a whole is a weighted average of the industry or sector profit shares. Since profit shares differ among industries and sectors, the aggregate profit share is therefore affected by the industry or sector composition of the economy.

Integrating some stylized facts of financialization and neoliberalism into this approach and reviewing the respective empirical literature, it can be argued that there is some convincing empirical evidence that financialization and neoliberalism have contributed to the rising gross profit share and hence to the falling labour income share since the early 1980s through three main channels:

First, the shift in the sector composition of the economy from the public sector and the non-financial business sector with higher labour income shares towards the financial business sector with a lower labour income share has contributed to the fall in the labour income share for the economy as a whole.

Second, the increase in management salaries as a part of overhead costs together with rising profit claims of the rentiers, i.e. rising interest and dividend payments of the corporate sector, have in sum been associated with a falling labour income share, although management salaries are part of compensation of employees in the national accounts and thus of the labour income share.

Third, financialization and neo-liberalism have weakened trade union bargaining power through several channels: increasing shareholder value and short-term profitability orientation of management, sector shifts away from the public sector and the non-financial business sector with stronger trade unions in many countries to the financial sector with weaker unions, abandonment of government demand management and full employment policies, deregulation of the labour market, and liberalisation and globalisation of international trade and finance.

These developments have not only triggered falling labour income shares, but they should have also been conducive to the observed increases in inequality of personal/household incomes.

Implications for shared prosperity

An agenda for shared prosperity, or a wage-led or mass income-led recovery strategy, would have to address the main causes for falling labour income shares and rising inequality in the period of neoliberalism and financialization: First, bargaining power of trade unions would have to be stabilised and enhanced by means of improving employment through active demand management policies, enlarging workers' and trade union rights, and reconstructing efficient wage bargaining institutions. Second, overhead costs of firms, in particular top management salaries and interest payments, as well as profit and dividend claims of financial wealth holders would have to be reduced. And third, the sector composition of the economy would have to be shifted away from the high profit share financial sector towards the non-financial corporate sector and the public sector.

Although reversing the trends in primary functional distribution is the key for a shared prosperity strategy, distribution policies should not only address functional income shares. The focus should also be on reducing inequality of personal distribution of income, in particular of disposable income. This means that the tendencies towards increasing wage dispersion have to be contained and, in particular, that progressive tax policies and social policies need to be applied in order to reduce inequality in the distribution of disposable income.

A wage-led or mass income-led recovery is the core of and should be embedded in a 'Keynesian New Deal at the Global (and the European) level' which more broadly would have to address the three main causes for the severity of the crisis: inefficient regulation of financial markets, the inequality in the distribution of income and the current account imbalances at the global (and at the euro area) level. As discussed in more detail in Hein/Truger (2012/13), the three main pillars of such a policy package are:

- First, the re-regulation and downsizing of the financial sector in order to prevent future financial excesses and financial crises, focusing on increasing transparency and reducing uncertainty, on generating incentives for long-run real investments, and on containing systemic instability.
- Second, the re-orientation of macroeconomic policies towards stimulating domestic demand, in particular in the current account surplus countries, through low interest rate monetary policies, functional finance fiscal policies and productivity-oriented wage policies.
- Third, the re-construction of international macroeconomic policy co-ordination (in particular in the euro area) and a new world financial order, which would have to focus on current account imbalances and on preventing 'beggar thy neighbour' policies.

References

Alvaredo, F., Atkinson, A.B., Piketty, T. and Saez, E. (2012), The World Top Incomes Database, http://g-mond.parisschoolofeconomics.eu/topincomes.

Atkinson, A.B. (2009), "Factor shares: the principal problem of political economy?" *Oxford Review of Economic Policy*, 25 (1), 3-16.

Bach, S., Corneo, G. and Steiner, V. (2009), "From bottom to top: the entire distribution of market income in Germany, 1992-2003", *Review of Income and Wealth*, 55, 303-330.

Buchele, R. and Christiansen, J. (2007), "Globalization and the declining share of labor income in the United States", paper prepared for the 28th International Working Party on Labor Market Segmentation, Aix-en-Provence, France, July 5-7, 2007, http://gesd.free.fr/paper419.pdf .

Dünhaupt, P. (2011), "Financialization, corporate governance and income distribution in the USA and Germany: introducing an adjusted wage share indicator", in T. Niechoj, Ö. Onaran, E. Stockhammer, A. Truger and T. van Treeck (eds.), *Stabilising an Unequal Economy? Public Debt, Financial Regulation, and Income Distribution*, Marburg, Metropolis.

European Commission (2010), AMECO Database, Spring 2010, http://ec.europa.eu/economy_finance/db_indicators/ameco/index_en.htm.

Glyn, A. (2009), "Functional distribution and inequality", in W. Salverda, B. Nolan and T.M. Smeeding (eds.), *The Oxford Handbook of Economy Inequality*, Oxford, Oxford University Press.

Hein, E. (2012), *The Macroeconomics of Finance-dominated Capitalism – and its Crisis*, Cheltenham, Edward Elgar.

Hein, E. (2013), "Finance-dominated capitalism and re-distribution of income – a Kaleckian perspective", *Cambridge Journal of Economics*, advance access, doi:10.1093/cje/bet038.

Hein, E., Mundt, M. (2012), "Financialisation and the requirements and potentials for wage-led recovery – a review focussing on the G20", Conditions of Work and Employment Series No. 37, Geneva, International Labour Organisation.

Hein, E., Truger, A. (2012/13), "Finance-dominated capitalism in crisis – the case for a global Keynesian New Deal", *Journal of Post Keynesian Economics*, 35, 183-210.

Kalecki, M. (1954), *Theory of Economic Dynamics*, London, George Allen and Unwin.

OECD (2012), OECD.StatExtracts, http,//stats.oecd.org/Index.aspx.

Palley, T. (2012), *From Crisis to Stagnation: The Destruction of Shared Prosperity and the Role of Economics*, Cambridge/UK, Cambridge University Press.

Palley, T. (2013), *Financialization: The Economics of Finance Capital Domination*, Basingstoke, Palgrave Macmillan.

Stiglitz, J. (2012), *The Price of Inequality. How Today's Divided Society Endangers Our Future*, New York, London, W.W. Norton & Company.

UNCTAD (2012), Trade and Development Report. Policies for Inclusive and Balanced Growth, New York, Geneva, United Nations.

20. Why the World Economy is Stuck With Flexible Labor Markets[*]

Heiner Flassbeck, P.h.D., *Professor, University of Hamburg and Director of Flassbeck-economics, hflassbeck@gmail.com*

Introduction

Flexibility of labor markets is the most important feature of the mantra of "structural policies" that are advocated in troubled countries after the big financial crisis. They were also the key message of the neoliberal revolution that overthrew Keynesianism and challenged the welfare state when unemployment rose during the 1970s.

Sometimes, it is also argued that globalization and technological change demands more wage flexibility in industrialized economies as labor is now under pressure from both lower paid workers in developing economies and labor saving technologies. However, a closer look at the evidence shows neither high unemployment nor international or structural changes justify a redistribution of income in favor of the rich and at the expense of the poor.

There are no natural or inevitable economic forces that compel modern societies to tolerate rising inequality caused by increased labor market flexibility. In fact, the belief that increased inequality is the outcome of an efficient market process in a world of high unemployment and rapid technological change is based on fundamental misunderstanding of how market economies work. This misunderstanding stems from mainstream economic theory. Replacing mainstream theory with a better understanding of market economies removes the conflict between wages and employment.

The dominance of mainstream economic theory is demonstrated by the fact that there is more and more critical discussion about the trend of rising inequality, yet the "structural" measures that are proposed by mainstream economists to overcome the crises triggered by the failure of financial markets involve wage cutting and stimulating investment by means of greater inequality. In fact, this policy pattern has ruled for most of the last thirty-five years, and it explains a huge amount of the increase in global income inequality, the increase in unemployment, and the increased frequency of crises. The traditional medicine of wage flexibility has worsened the problem of inequality without healing the problem of unemployment. Revamping

---

[*] This paper draws from Chapter V of the Trade and Development Report of UNCTAD of 2012, which was authored by Heiner Flassbeck.

mainstream theory is not enough: only a new theoretical approach and a totally different therapy can restore health.

Imagine a world in which the labor market is initially in equilibrium and a shock outside of labor markets causes unemployment to rise. The resulting surplus supply of labor would then put downward pressure on the price of labor, causing wages and salaries to fall. However, falling wages would then depress demand for most products of this economy, further damping the willingness of companies to hire workers despite low or even falling wages. The clear implication is that the traditional recipe of workers trying to price themselves back into employment by accepting wage cuts, cannot work because lower wages simply further reduce overall demand. Far from solving the problem, wage reduction actually worsens problem and destabilizes the economy. In a situation of demand shortage, what is needed is an increase in aggregate demand, not a reduction.

The idea that high wages are the cause of current unemployment is implausible. The financial crisis of 2008 was a shock from outside the labor market. Despite the wage share of GDP in developed economies being at its lowest level since the Second World War, unemployment shot up in 2008/2009 to a level of 9 per cent, marking the highest level in the history of the last sixty years.

Since the beginning of the "Great Recession" in 2009, unemployment has once again become the global economy's most pressing economic problem. According to neoclassical economic theory this should not have happened, as the shock was financial and not a shock to the real productive capacities of the economy. Moreover, the fact that the wage share of GDP was already extremely low is *prima facie* evidence against the idea of wages being the cause mass unemployment. The fact that unemployment has risen to higher levels than in any other recession in the last three decades despite the wage share being far lower, proves that something must be wrong with the underlying theory.

The return of the old model

The return of the pre-Keynesian economics of the 1920s was fuelled by the fact that unemployment rose in the 1970s in tandem with a rising wage share. According to pre-Keynesian theory, the unwillingness of workers to accept lower wages in face of changed circumstances at the level of the firm is the root cause of unemployment. Consequently, too little inequality and the resistance of unions to the "need" for lower wages became increasingly identified as the main culprit for emergence of a persistent unemployment problem in the 1970s.

Among the international institutions, it was mainly the OECD (OECD 1994) that championed the revival of this pre-Keynesian approach. Its recommendations justified the adoption of so-called labor market flexibility policies, which go a long way to explaining rising inequality in the developed world over the last three decades. In its famous *Jobs Study* of 1994, the OECD describes the labor market adjustment mechanism leading to superior employment outcomes as follows:

"The adjustment process itself depends on the interplay of employers' demand for labour, which will be negatively related to the level of real wages, and the desire to be employed, which will be positively related to the level of real wages. In principle, there will be a real wage level – or, more correctly, a level of real labour costs – that ensures that all who want to work at that wage will find employment."(Part I, p. 69)

And elsewhere:

"Self-equilibration in the labour market requires, in addition to a negative relationship between labour-demand and labour costs, that wages respond to market conditions: labour-market slack putting downward pressure on real wages and vice versa." (Part II, p. 3)

As mentioned above, whatever the reasons for the rise in unemployment, the huge increase in unemployment put enormous pressure on wages by tilting the balance of negotiating power towards employers. When threatened by unemployment, workers are normally willing to sacrifice their share of productivity increases, or even relinquish previous wage gains in order to secure their jobs. However, what looks like a stabilizing adjustment at the level of the individual firm or individual industrial sector, is a destabilizing force for the overall economy. Whereas a supply surplus in goods markets induces a fall in price that helps demand, a fall in the price of labor in response to unemployment worsens the problem when unemployment is due to demand shortage.

Consider the United States. Wages lagged productivity for many years before the crisis and the median wages of workers had not increased significantly for almost three decades. When the crisis hit in 2008 and 2009, unemployment rose at least as sharply as in former recessions, and it seems to be even more persistent than in prior recessions. But if unemployment can rise sharply despite real wages lagging behind productivity for decades, which suggests the conventional assertion of a nexus between real wages and employment does not apply. Moreover, it suggests that lowering wages to increase employment and reduce unemployment is not warranted.

Today, there is growing doubt whether cutting wages in countries like the US would improve the employment situation. Wouldn't companies adjust their production further downwards if the effect of a fall in nominal wages was to reduce demand of most private households?

The crucial point is the sequence of events. Economists tend to tell the result of wages adjusting downwards in a recession from the point of view of given supply and demand schedules with normal price elasticities. But *a priori* belief in the logic of normal supply and demand curves cannot guide a proper judgment for labor as a whole. In an economy evolving over time under the conditions of objective uncertainty - the state of non-ergodic development, as it is called by Paul Davidson (Davidson 2013), - no single player has meta-information concerning the outcome of complex processes that would allow him to react differently than others in case of external or exogenous shocks.

Consider a general fall of (nominal) wages triggered by recession and rising unemployment. Expecting that lower nominal wages will also reduce income in real terms, private households would immediately reduce their consumption in an attempt to avoid a deterioration of their balance sheets. For employers, at first glance, falling wages helps restore profits, which are pressured in recession by falling demand. However, if falling demand from private households further depresses their business and puts additional downward pressure on prices and demand, the relief from lower wages is a mixed blessing. Faced with more pressure on prices and falling demand during the recession the average firm will refrain from taking strategic decisions on the further use of labor and capital. To expect that in the middle of a recession the average firm engages in a restructuring process favoring labor against capital, as foreseen by the neoclassical approach of employment theory, is naïve to say the least.

Falling nominal wages that signal for every individual firm a lasting fall of real wages and a lasting change in relative prices of labor and capital, thereby inducing firms to alter the production process by substituting capital for labor, is a mere fiction. Such a process, in addition to being applied by all firms at the same time, would have to be extremely speedy. Only a more or less timeless transition from one production structure to the other would prevent overall demand from falling.

Falling demand fundamentally alters the conditions under which firms adjust to the change in relative prices of the factors of production. If wages per hour fall and the growth in the number of hours worked do not make up exactly for the fall in wages, the wage sum for the economy will fall and, with very high probability, induce falling demand.

A similar argument has to be made concerning some less sophisticated theoretical ideas that assume a simple shift of income from wages to profits as a result of falling wages. However, such a shift as a consequence of falling nominal wages can only occur if it is assumed that overall demand remains unchanged. However, this will not be the case. Once again the sequence of events is crucial. If demand decreases immediately after the drop in wages[1] the expected substitution of falling wages by higher profits is impossible due to the fall in overall output. Only a drop in the saving ratio of workers, private households in general or increased deficits of the government could prevent the immediate reduction of demand and the subsequent reduction in profits.

Obviously, this analysis is only valid for closed economies; it is less clear-cut for open economies in which exports are an important share of overall demand. Exports may expand in reaction to wage cuts under certain circumstances. If wages are cut in one country only, its exports may increase as long as it labor productivity is unchanged and its currency does not revalue in a way that the fall in wages is offset. However, the overall effect on total demand depends on the relative weights of domestic demand compared to exports. For very open economies the net effect may be positive. Moreover, improved competitiveness can have a lasting effect on export demand as the country gains market shares and thus benefits even further from global demand growth. On the other hand, continued real depreciation by means of wage cuts may massively distort international trade and create huge payments imbalances as the effects on competitiveness accumulate and create a huge absolute advantage for the country over time.

However, the bigger a country and the larger are its exports and imports within the global economy, the less that country will be able to sustain a policy of appropriating global market share through wage cuts. Its trading partners will start retaliating via measures such as cutting their own wages, forcing a depreciation of their exchange rate, erecting protectionist trade barriers.

The crucial nexus for sustainable success in open and in closed economies is between money wages (nominal wages) and employment. Only money wages rising strictly in line with the productivity trend plus the inflation target can assure that the economy as a whole creates a sufficient amount of demand to fully employ its human and its technical capacities. The wage share remains constant in such an approach and cannot correct for years of wage restraint in the past.

---

[1] Demand could even fall before wages actually come down. If such a measure is broadly discussed among union members or accompanied by strikes and demonstrations private households may cut their demand in advance to accommodate the expected wage cut.

Growth, not real wages determines employment

The implications of this analysis are crucial for economic policy. The simple supply-demand apparatus cannot be applied to the labor market for the economy as a whole, which means a rise in unemployment cannot be avoided by flexible wages. The creation of new employment is a positive function of output growth, not of falling wages and a deteriorating wage share. To analyse the labor market in isolation without relating it to the overall flow of income is a grave error.

For most countries in the world, but especially for developed countries, employment cycles are very closely associated with cycles of output growth. That explains why a downswing like the "Great Recession" of 2008 and 2009 destroyed employment despite wage flexibility and very low wage shares.

The fact that macroeconomic environments have evolved over time in different ways is due to different macroeconomic approaches rather than to different degrees of wage flexibility among similar countries. There can be no doubt that the years of rather high employment growth during the 1970s and the 1980s were years of much less wage restraint than the last two decades. Yet, the last two decades showed meagre employment gains compared with the former.

Given the rate of productivity growth, the growth of aggregate demand sufficient to create employment for all persons willing to work, depends on the distribution of the gains from productivity growth. The policies adopted over the past 25 years have sought to keep wages low, and have served to translate productivity gains either into higher capital income or lower output prices. But, as shown above, suppressing wages in order to generate higher profits is self-defeating. Without rising purchasing power of wage earners, the demand growth needed to utilize existing capacity does not materialize.

The only escape is stimulation of foreign demand through falling wages and an improved competitiveness, but this creates a fallacy of composition. Competitiveness is a relative concept: not all countries can improve their competitiveness at the same time. Employment creation at the expense of growth and employment generation in other countries creates unsustainable debt accumulation in the deficit countries.

For the world as a whole - as well as for any single and rather large country over the medium term - real wages rising in line with productivity growth is indispensible to generate an amount of domestic effective demand that will fully utilize the capacities and thereby nourish a virtuous cycle of growth, investment, productivity increases and employment.

If dysfunctional flexibility of nominal wages at the level of the overall economy is avoided and nominal wages in all countries broadly follow the golden growth rule described above (nominal wages growing in line with average productivity growth plus an inflation target) the wage share remains constant and most groups of society will fully participate in society's economic progress. In this case, the overall growth of nominal unit labour-costs (ULC) equals the inflation rate. For the developed countries this was true for long periods of history, and in particular for those periods where the creation of jobs was rapid and unemployment fell.

The participation of the majority of the people is crucial for success because their growing income is the main source of consumption of domestically produced goods and services. Only if the proceeds of productive activity are channelled through the pockets of all income groups can society at large expect dynamics of investment in a broad range of activities and the emergence of a diversified economy in the long run.

Income growth and employment undoubtedly depend on investment in fixed capital. In economies with a dominant private sector, such investment is strongly influenced by the growth of demand for the goods and services and on the provision of finance to pay for such investment. Public policies must support investment on both sides – the demand side and the finance side.

Economic Policy is key for employment growth

Flexibility of the labor market is the mantra of the neoliberal counter-revolution of the last decades. It is predicated on a model of the economy that does not resemble the world we live in. In reality, there is no static equilibrium on the labor market that can be restored after a shock by means of flexible wages. Efficient dynamic adjustment to shocks in an economy living under conditions of objective uncertainty is fundamentally different. It must take into account that the preferences and the income of the majority of the population are not only the main purpose of the system, but also the main drivers. In such an approach the notion of flexibility loses its fascination.

At the macro level, the use of flexible wages and increased inequality as a remedy for unemployment is definitively ineffective if the economy confronts a demand shock. While huge macro-economically relevant supply shocks like an oil price shock require some kind of passive flexibility on the side of workers, the traditionally propagated micro or sector flexibility of wages and the implied redistribution is ineffective against demand shocks.

Flexible profits rather than flexible wages fit the dynamics of modern market systems. In the real world shocks are mainly absorbed by profits and not by wages, which applies to all sorts of shocks, including from foreign trade and foreign direct investment. By changing profits the economy is given the direction it needs to face the next challenge instead of restoring the unrestorable. The static neoclassical model of separated labor markets with flexible wages that regularly produce inequality in case of adjustment to shocks, be they international or inter-temporal, is not relevant and should not guide the policies of adjustment at any stage of development.

Protecting workers against the permanent pressure to "price themselves back into the market" (OECD) is crucial for successful adjustment. Measures to protect workers from psychological harm and damage to their skills from prolonged unemployment are important in their own right, but they are also critical as part of ensuring the stable adjustment of the economic system. To prevent the "pass through" of high unemployment to wages following shocks on the goods or financial markets, there is need for a robust safety net that allows temporarily unemployed workers to search for jobs elsewhere in the economy without taking major cuts in their standard of living.

Governments that quickly and aggressively tackle rising unemployment can reduce both the uncertainty and threat for individual workers and the danger of a second recessionary dip owing to the pressure of increased unemployment on wages and domestic demand. Indeed, in the US a more aggressive stance of economic policy in recessions has long been seen as a substitute to a more advanced social safety net such as in Europe, with its more generous and extensive unemployment insurance.

In sum, cuts in wages and rising inequality are an ineffective instrument for dealing with rising unemployment, and government is need to prevent the negative externalities that come from falling wages. Governments can prevent huge additional costs that arise if the pressure on wages, stemming from high unemployment, is allowed to permeate the economy. The negative second round effects of falling wages or the wage share on domestic demand can and should be avoided.

This result must sound perplexing to those who have grown up with the conventional supply and demand approach to labor markets. However, even for the believers in the logic of supply and demand, the fact that unemployment has risen enormously throughout the developed world without any increase in the wage share and when the wage share was already low, should be cause to reflect on their position. If the labor market can be dislodged so easily from "equilibrium" without a shock to the labor market (i.e. by a financial crisis), there is no reason to believe that falling wages will restore lower unemployment.

References

Davidson P (2013), Uncertainty and Austerity Policy, in: H. Flassbeck, P., Davidson, J.K. Galbraith, R. Koo and J. Ghosh (2013), *Economic Reform Now*, Palgrave Macmillan.

Flassbeck H (2001). The Exchange Rate: Economic Policy Tool or Market Price? UNCTAD Discussion Paper 157, Geneva. November.

Keynes JM (1936). *The General Theory of Employment, Interest and Money*. London and Basingstoke: Macmillan and Cambridge University Press for the Royal Economic Society.

OECD (1994). *The OECD Jobs Study*. Paris.

UNCTAD (United Nations Conference on Trade and Development) (2011). Trade and Development Report: Post-crisis policy challenges in the world economy. New York and Geneva.

UNCTAD (2012). Trade and Development Report: Policies for Inclusive and Balanced Growth. New York and Geneva.

21. Low Wages in Germany and the European Imbalance Problem

Gerhard Bosch, Professor at the University Duisburg-Essen and Director of the Institut Arbeit und Qualifikation (Institute for Work, Skills and Training), gerhard.bosch@uni-due.de.

A misdiagnosis becomes prevailing opinion

Germany has achieved annual trade surpluses, with few exceptions, since the 1950s. Prior to the introduction of the euro there was need for regular upward revaluations of the deutschmark to correct for theses surpluses. However, the introduction of the euro meant exchange-rate adjustments within the eurozone were no longer available as a corrective measure. Furthermore, because a substantial number of eurozone nations were running trade deficits, that offset Germany's trade surpluses and removed pressure for upward revaluation of the euro.

These two features have helped protect Germany's competitive export position. On top of that, Germany's competitive position has been further enhanced since the late 1990s as a result of below-average wage increases relative to other eurozone countries, which in effect amounted to an internal devaluation within the euro zone. This contributed to further a rise in German export surpluses, which by 2012 were equivalent to about 6.5% of the German gross national product. In other words, over a three-year period Germany is forced to invest about 20% of its GNP overseas. German surpluses are matched by corresponding deficits in other eurozone countries. Currently, the German economy finds itself in an exceptional situation in Europe as a result of its highly developed international trade links. The openness of the economy (total of exports and imports as a proportion of GNP) in Germany, France, Spain and Italy was about 50% in 1995. However, by 2008 the figure for Germany was approximately 90%, compared to only 60% in the other countries Joebges et al. (2010: 6).

One of the paradoxes of the economic policy debate in Germany is that the most serious weaknesses are perceived to be in precisely those areas in which Germany is particularly strong. Thus, competitiveness is the dominant issue while the problem of strengthening of domestic demand has disappeared from the agenda. For 20 years now, German economic policy has been driven by a one-sided concentration on exports and the aspiration to improve the competitiveness of German industry. The politically powerful employers' associations are dominated by those representing manufacturing industry, where the aim is to enhance global market share by keeping wages low. A large-scale media campaign mounted by the 'Initiative Neue Soziale Marktwirtschaft' (New Social Market Economy Initiative) – which has been funded since 2000 by the employer organisations in the metalworking and electrical industries – has successfully propagated the view that Germany, for all its low wage increases and large export surpluses, suffers from high labor costs and inflexible labor market regulations, and is consequently uncompetitive.

Those who subscribed to this view included the first Red-Green coalition. The Hartz legislation of 2004 was aimed at giving Germany a low-wage sector. By reducing unemployment pay – previously means-tested – for the long-term unemployed to the lower social benefit level, and by re-setting the 'reasonableness' criteria, the Hartz reforms stepped up pressure on the unemployed to accept work with pay as much as 30% below the going rate for their locality. Deregulation of temporary agency work and of so-called mini-jobs[1] made it possible to replace employees on standard contracts with replacements on precarious contracts. In the case of temporary agency work, contracts ceased to be time-limited, and a new mechanism involving wage agreements enabled employers to sidestep the principle that temporary staff would have equal pay with the hiring company's regular employees. As for 'mini-jobs', the income threshold was raised and mini-jobs were also allowed as a second job. The cap on permissible hours worked per week was also lifted, enabling wage rates to be reduced. The Hartz legislation's political acceptability rested on the assertion that low-skilled employees with low productivity would benefit the most from expanding the low-wage sector.

The low-wage sector in Germany

Since the end of the 1990s, German wages have risen less than those in the rest of the EU. One principal reason for this is the rapid expansion of the low-wage sector, which was under way before the Hartz reforms. The share of low-wage workers (less than 2/3 of the median hourly wage) rose from 17.7% in 1995 to 23.1% of all workers in 2010. The number of low-wage workers increased from 5.6 million in 1995 to 7.9 million in 2010. One particularity of the German low-wage sector is its marked downward dispersion, since there is no minimum wage to prevent very low wages. In 2010, 6.8 million workers were paid less than the minimum wage of 8.50 euros demanded by the German Trade Union Federation, while 2.5 million

---

[1] *Minijobs* are jobs carrying a maximum monthly wage of 450€. Those holding them are exempt from tax and other deductions. Employers are required to make a flat-rate 30% contribution. Under European and German legislation, holders of mini-jobs are entitled to the same pay for the same work and also to paid holidays, including statutory holidays, and paid sick leave.

actually earned even less than 6.00 euros per hour (Kalina and Weinkopf, 2012).

Virtually all the growth in absolute terms took place in West Germany (i.e. in areas traditionally protected by high levels of adherence to collective agreements). Examination of the evolution of the inflation-adjusted wage distribution since 1995 shows that the concentration of wages around the mid-point of the wage distribution is crumbling and many previously well-paid activities are sliding downwards (see Figure 1).

Figure 1: Distribution of hourly pay, German, adjusted for inflation (base = 1995)

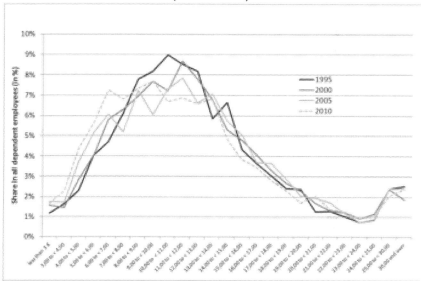

Source: SOEP 2012, calculations by the IAQ, Thorsten Kalina

Low-wage work is not equally distributed among all employees. In 2010, those particularly affected by low wages were younger employees under 25 (50.8%), those on fixed-term contracts (45.7%), those without vocational training (39.3%), women (30.0%) and foreigners (31.9%) (see Table 1). Because of the variable size of these employee categories, a distinction must be made between the impact on individual groups and the composition of the low-wage working population. Thus in 2010, 30% of female employees were paid low wages, but they accounted for almost two thirds (63.7%) of all low-paid workers (see Table 1). One particularity of the German low-wage sector, compared to the US, is the high share of employees with a vocational qualification. In Germany around 80% of people in the sector have a vocational or higher education qualification which is far above the US level

(Bosch and Weinkopf, 2008). The Hartz reforms' aim of improving the employment chances of low-skill workers has not been fulfilled.

Table 1: Share of low-wage work and share of low-wage sector by employee category (Germany, all dependent employees, excl. school pupils, students and pensioners, in %)

	Category	Share of LW workers in category		Share in LW sector	
		1995	2010	1995	2010
Qualification	No vocational qualification	25.8	39.3	22.4	18.4
	Vocational qualification	17.0	24.7	67.2	71.0
	HE qualification	9.5	10.9	10.4	10.6
Gender	Men	10.8	16.7	37.6	36.3
	Women	26.0	30.0	62.4	63.7
Age	Under 25	34.9	50.8	13.6	11.2
	25 – 34	16.7	23.6	28.0	20.4
	35 – 44	14.7	20.3	23.7	23.1
	45 – 54	14.7	19.2	20.4	25.1
	55+	17.8	26.2	14.2	20.3
Nationality	German	17.0	22.6	90.6	88.7
	Foreign	17.2	30.6	9.4	11.3
Employment contract	Fixed-term	26.9	45.7	9.5	20.7
	Open-ended	16.2	18.9	90.5	79.3
Working time	Full-time	13.9	15.5	65.8	47.6
	Part-time (liable for social insurance contributions)	19.5	26.6	18.3	24.0
	Mini-job	77.1	86.1	16.0	28.4

Source: SOEP 2010, calculations by the IAQ (Thorsten Kalina).
* = <two thirds of the median hourly rate of pay

Factors causing the expansion of low-wage work

The expansion of the low-wage sector began around 10 years before the Hartz reforms. The causes were changes in the behavior of employers. First, many employers took advantage of high unemployment to quit employers' associations and thereby cease being bound by collective agreements. Second, the opening up of many previously public services (post, railways, local transport etc.) to private providers meant the entry of new firms who were not bound by collective agreement and competed with state-owned companies by engaging in wage dumping.

The Hartz reforms did not initiate this process, but they did prevent low-wage work from being reduced in the strong upturn from 2005 onwards. That is because the two deregulated employment forms, temporary agency work and mini-jobs, gained considerably in importance. The number of temporary agency workers rose from 300,000 in 2003 to around 900,000 in 2011, while over the same period the number of people employed in mini-jobs rose from around 5.5 million to 7.5 million. Among employees in mini-jobs, the share of low-wage workers was 86% in 2010 (Table 2). According to another survey, it was around two thirds for temporary agency workers.

The high share of low-wage work among mini-jobbers can be explained primarily by the fact that employees in these jobs are generally, and in contravention of the European directive on the equal treatment of part-time workers, paid less than other part-timers. As far as temporary agency workers are concerned, the equal pay principle of the European directive on temporary work has been abrogated by collective agreements that amount to wage dumping concluded by the employer-friendly Christian trade union that has virtually no members.

The increase in low-wage work was supposed to make it easier for unemployed individuals to enter the labor market and to improve the employment chances of low-skill workers. In the mid-1990s, the German labor market was still being praised by the OECD for the good opportunities for advancement it offered low wage earners (OECD, 1996). That has now fundamentally changed. More recent investigations show that low-wage work is becoming increasingly entrenched. Kalina (2012) shows that chances of advancement declined over the long period between 1975/6 and 2005/6. Mosthaf et al. (2011) note that only about one in every seven full-time workers who were low paid in 1998/9 was able to leave the low-wage sector by 2007.

Deregulating the labor market has had no effect on employment levels

Coverage by collective agreement, which was around 80% prior to 1990, but by 2010 it had declined to 60% in West Germany and 48% in East Germany. Autonomous wage-setting by the social partners is obviously no longer functioning. In many small and medium-sized enterprises and service industries, wages are determined unilaterally by employers since collective agreements are not in force and works councils have not been set up.

As a result, the trade unions have reconsidered their rejection of state intervention in the wage-setting process, and since the Hartz reforms unions have been campaigning for the introduction of minimum wages. Industry minimum wages have now been agreed with employers' associations in 12 industries and have been declared generally binding by the Federal Government.

The effects of minimum wages on pay levels and employment have been investigated in eight industries, in some cases using a difference in differences estimation. No negative employment effects were observed (Bosch and Weinkopf, 2012). However, a trend change towards a reduction in low-wage employment has not yet been instigated since the largest low-wage sectors, such as retailing and hotels and catering, do not have industry minimum wages. Attempts to introduce a national minimum wage and reform the Collective Bargaining Act to make it easier to declare industry agreements generally binding have so far been blocked by opposition at the federal government level.

The most contentious effects of the Hartz reforms are those on employment levels. Their positive employment effects are often explained in terms of higher outflows from unemployment since 2005. However, since inflows into unemployment have increased at the same time, despite the economic upturn, flows between both employment and unemployment have increased. The reason for the increased flows in the economic upturn is the increased use of fixed-term contracts and temporary agency work, which often leads to short periods of employment.

The Hartz legislation came into force just as Germany was coming out of a deep recession. In the subsequent upturn, there was a sharp cyclical increase in employment. If the Hartz reforms did indeed influence this positive employment trend, then either the upturn must have been more employment–intensive as a result of better matching processes or the upturn was accelerated by the Hartz reforms. Horn and Herzog-Stein (2012) have compared the employment intensity of three economic cycles (1999/Q1 – 2001/Q1, 2005/Q2 – 2008/Q1 and 2009/Q2 until the current end point). In the first upturn, employment intensity (i.e. the percentage increase in the level of gainful employment when GDP rises by 1%) was 0.43% and in the two subsequent upturns it was just 0.35% and 0.39% respectively. Their findings show that employment intensity actually weakened after the Hartz reforms. The reality is that the two upturns after the Hartz reforms came into force were almost wholly driven by exports. The Hartz reforms had a damping effect on the evolution of wages. However, since this effect was concentrated primarily in the service sector, its impact was to dampen domestic demand and demand for imports, but it had little effect on the export sector.

Germany shares the responsibility of stimulating European economic growth

The above evidence shows that the favorable evolution of employment in Germany in recent years has nothing to do with the Hartz reforms. Instead, it is the result of German manufacturing industry's specialization, acquired over many years, in high-quality products, driven by a rapid pace of innovation, above-average investment in R&D, and a good vocational training system. Moreover, Germany's product portfolio, with its emphasis on capital goods and cars, was well matched to the sharply increasing demand from the BRICS and other developing countries. That meant the German economy was not wholly dependent on the European market.

The principle contribution of the Hartz reforms was that they enabled Germany, even in the strong upturn of 2005 to 2008, to continue its policy of internal devaluation within the Eurozone by means of below-average wage increases and unit wage costs relative to other Eurozone countries (Stein, Stephan, and Zwiener, 2012). Since domestic demand and imports did not keep pace with the growth of exports, trade imbalances within the Eurozone increased. This is one of the principal reasons for the Euro crisis, and the Hartz reforms are therefore implicated as a contributing cause of the crisis.

German economic policy continues to be characterized by an excessive focus on exports. As a way of dealing with the euro crisis, the German federal government advises other countries to introduce their own labor market reforms on the model of the Hartz Acts. This policy, however, cannot be applied at will to other countries, since only by abolishing the laws of mathematics would be it possible for all countries to have export surpluses.

Indisputably, the Southern European nations need to improve their competitiveness. But the crisis engulfing the euro can only be overcome if Germany, the strongest economy in Europe, takes responsibility for generating growth. A two prong strategy can accomplish this. The first prong focuses on the labor market and would aim to restore health to Germany's remuneration system by introducing a minimum wage and strengthening existing wage agreements. The second prong would increase public investment in Germany, preferably under the aegis of a European investment program. This would reverse the decline in net public investment that has occurred over the last decade

References

Bosch, G. and Weinkopf, C. (eds.) (2008), *Low-wage Work in Germany*, New York: Russell Sage Foundation.

Bosch, G. and Weinkopf, C. (2012), Wirkungen der Mindestlohnregelungen in acht Branchen, Expertise im Auftrag der FES, Bonn (Effects of minimum-wage regulations in eight sectors. Expert report commissioned by FES, Bonn)

Horn, G. A. and Herzog-Stein, A. (2012), "Erwerbstätigenrekord dank guter Konjunktur und hoher interner Flexibilität" (Record employment figures owed to upswing and high internal flexibility), *Wirtschaftsdienst*, no. 3, pp. 151-155

Joebges, H., Logeay, C., Stephan, S., and Zwiener, R. (2010), "Deutschlands Exportüberschüsse gehen zu Lasten der Beschäftigten" (Germany's export surpluses are being paid for by the workforce), WISO Diskurs, pp. 1-35.

Kalina, T. (2012), Niedriglohnbeschäftigte in der Sackgasse ? – Was die Segmentationstheorie zum Verständnis des Niedriglohnsektors in Deutschland beitragen kann (Low-wage workers at a dead-end? How segmentation theory can contribute to understanding the low-wage sector in Germany). Diss. Duisburg, Univ. DU-E.

Mosthaf, A., Schnabel, C., and Stephani, J. (2010), Low-wage careers: are there dead-end firms and dead-end jobs? (Universität Erlangen, Nürnberg, Lehrstuhl für Arbeitsmarkt- und Regionalpolitik. Diskussionspapiere, 66), Nürnberg.

OECD (1996), *Employment Outlook*, Paris.

Stein, U., Stephan, S., and Zwiener, R. (2012), Zu schwache deutsche Arbeitskostenentwicklung belastet Europäische Währungsunion und soziale Sicherung, Arbeits- und Lohnstückkosten in 2011 und im 1. Halbjahr 2012 (Weak German labour costs development is putting strain on European Monetary Union and social security. Labour and unit wage costs in 2011 and first half 2012). Reihe IMK Report, Nr. 77.

22. Increasing and Sharing Prosperity Through Social Growth

Michael Dauderstädt, former Director of the Division for Economic and Social Policy of the Friedrich-Ebert Foundation (FES), Bonn, Germany, michael@dauderstaedt.de.

1. Social failings of the existing growth model

Prosperity is more than just monetary income and the consumption of goods and services which can be bought with that income on the market. It also includes leisure time, a healthy environment, decent work and access to public goods and services such as security, justice, and social protection. Shared prosperity implies that all citizens (or even all humankind) are provided with at least a minimum of all these benefits.

With regard to monetary income, still easily the most important component, this requires a more equal distribution of income. But equality must be extended to the other dimensions of welfare, too. In accordance with basic principles of democracy, equal rights should include not only equality before the law and equal political rights, but also equal life opportunities.

The currently dominant growth model, which was established in the early 1980s, has not delivered equal prosperity. Its market focus prioritizes growth of GDP and considers all other forms of prosperity as dependent on the success of the corporate sector, particularly its competitiveness and export performance. These other characteristics of prosperity are viewed as a luxury that only the market-strong can afford, rather than as an equally important output of societal production which is valuable in its own right and is also a crucial pre-condition of sustainable market production.

Not only has the current jaundiced growth model ignored these non-monetary characteristics of prosperity, it has also worsened income distribution in almost all OECD countries.[1] Moreover, the abandonment of the growth process to market forces has also created unsustainable developments. Income inequality has increased due to partial rolling back of the state and liberalization of labor markets. This was compounded by the fact that the growth process was led by financial markets, leading to an explosive increase in financial assets and corresponding debts. Internationally, this development took the form of large imbalances in international trade and capital movements. Over the years, these high current account surpluses and deficits have generated a high level of exposure and foreign debts. Together

---

[1] OECD: *Divided We Stand*, Paris 2011.

with public debt, which has increased sharply since the crisis, this has produced debt levels that now appear no longer sustainable. Debt reduction strategies are therefore called for that will entail a reversal of current capital flows. However, the burden of adjustment cannot be borne by the deficit countries alone; the surplus countries – and Germany in particular – must also participate.

Social growth – a model of a Progressive Economic Policy[2]

The concept of »social growth« presented here is the Friedrich-Ebert-Stiftung's (FES) proposal for a progressive economic policy model. The aim is to develop a growth model that combines prosperity for all with sustainability and justice. Its primary target is Germany, but it is also applicable to Europe and globally.

Although the progressive economic policy proposed here is focused directly on overcoming the economic and social crisis by means of social and, therefore, fairly structured growth, its indirect aim is to alleviate the environmental and political crisis in which Germany, Europe and the world find themselves.

Social growth, with its focus on education, health, care and climate protection, puts less pressure on natural resources than the conventional market-driven growth model. It also delivers the results that people expect from democratic politics, namely jobs and a share in the prosperity these jobs create. In this way, social growth confers legitimacy on democracy that seems to have been lost, not so much because of mistrust in its procedures, but rather the paucity of socially acceptable outcomes – in other words, states' inability to govern markets in the interests of society.

The goal of the social growth model proposed here is a change of course in economic policy combined with bolstering of domestic demand. Future growth, in particular employment growth, in Germany is likely to be primarily in services rather than manufacturing. There is a great deal of catching up to do, especially in social services such as education, health and care. Many needs, in particular those of low and middle income earners, cannot be satisfied because of a lack of purchasing power by those earners. That is why a new social, macroeconomically viable, structurally coherent and equitable growth model is needed. Such a model can absorb the unemployed or the underemployed in a growing service sector with decent work; increase employment and productivity; and improve income distribution.

---

[2] This text is based on a wealth of studies and reflections that have emerged in recent years either within the FES or commissioned by it – partly in the course of the project »Germany 2020« (2007–2009), partly within the framework of its successor project »Social Growth« which has been published under the title "Social growth – a model of a Progressive Economic Policy" (http://library.fes.de/pdf-files/id/ipa/08836.pdf).

»Social growth« is intended to offer as many people as possible an opportunity for decent work and a share in social prosperity. Needless to say, one can only distribute what has been produced – but people should also receive their fair share. The scope for improved distribution created by rising employment and productivity, should not only be used for more private and public consumption and investment, but also more free time. That includes shorter working weeks, more vacations and a longer safeguarded retirement. More jobs and productivity increases require investment in tangible and intangible capital stock, including human capital. These social investments must be promoted, channeled and liberated from the financial market casino.

Work, Productivity, Investment

On the supply side, economic growth results from more work and/or higher productivity. Both arise primarily from more investment, which either creates new jobs or modernizes the capital stock which makes labor more productive. However, these key growth factors require a more precise definition if they are to merit the predicate »good« or »social«.

Labor input should consist of decent work. Decent work is work that is properly paid, thereby enabling working people to provide adequately for themselves and their families. It also allows employees to have a say in their workplaces. These conditions are best fulfilled with full employment since that gives wage earners greater market power. However, it should be noted that additional employment that replaces undeclared »black« work (i.e. home or voluntary work) creates new prosperity only to the extent that it is more productive.

Social productivity differs from productivity as traditionally understood and measured in that it takes account of (negative) external effects and excludes increases in efficiency achieved at the expense of the employees. The value of a product – good or service – expresses a social need. Value creation can also result from improvements in quality from the consumer's standpoint. Apparent productivity increases achieved solely by means of higher output or lower input prices, work intensification (in other words, more work in the same time), a concealed reduction in quality, or an orientation towards an elitist demand structure resulting from unequal income distribution do not increase aggregate social wealth.

Social investments are expenditures that generate growth either by creating jobs or increasing productivity. Restructuring of assets between different financial investment vehicles does not count. Besides the traditional investments of private entrepreneurs in better capital stock, and thus in new or more productive jobs, government spending is not only in »bricks and mortar« (in other words, infrastructure) but also in education, research and health counts.

Social growth will take place predominantly through the expansion of service provision, especially in areas such as education, care and health. Here, too, growth will result, on the one hand, from additional employment and, on the other, from higher productivity. The new jobs will partly absorb the unemployed or those involuntarily working only part-time, and will partly originate from transforming services provided within the family into market services. This increases GDP, although social prosperity increases only to the extent that market-oriented work is more professional, more productive and of higher quality. It was long feared that services productivity cannot really increase (known as »Baumol's cost disease«). However, this thesis neglects important productivity components, such as quality and intangible capital.

Demand and Distribution

Social growth requires – like every stable and sustainable growth process – adequate development of aggregate demand. Social demand is constrained by the aggregate of incomes, state transfers and additional lending. Incomes have an impact on demand only if they are either spent directly or are diverted via the state – taxes and contributions – or via the financial sector to those who spend them. As a rule, the money diverted via the state is spent since both the recipients of transfer payments and the state as provider of public goods barely save. Concerning the savings made available to the financial sector things are more problematic since they can flow into investment vehicles that do little to stimulate the real economy. However, the financial sector – especially when the central bank's monetary policy is accommodating – can also create loans beyond the savings of other actors (mainly households, but also companies and, rarely, the state). Only these loans, which exceed savings, feed growth.

Growth requires that sectors or actors are willing to incur debt and thus to absorb the savings of other actors or sectors. Without this willingness to incur debt growth would grind to a halt since otherwise increasing supply would not find sufficient demand, other than via falling prices. This willingness depends on the interest rate. Interest rates must be lower than expected returns. With regard to the economy as a whole, however, the central bank must select the interest rate in such a way that the resulting total lending and corresponding demand do not greatly exceed real supply opportunities and create excessive inflation.

For a while, borrowing can compensate for a lack of demand owing to low wages, as happened in the United States in the years before the outbreak of the financial crisis in 2007. However, the US example shows that escalating debt cannot be a sustainable substitute for too low and unequally distributed incomes. High incomes lead to a high savings rate. In Germany and many other countries income distribution in the past twenty years has become markedly more unequal. This has not only dampened demand but has caused the emergence of a demand structure increasingly oriented towards the interests of wealthier households (luxury and positional goods). This trend was reinforced by the diminishing tax burden on wealthier households. These tax breaks also limited the capacity of the state to satisfy social needs for public goods and services. In future, therefore, it must be ensured that additional value creation is also shared by employees. Only in this way can weak demand be prevented from hindering growth.

Affordable equal prosperity

It is often said, mostly by conservatives, that today's economies and societies cannot afford generous welfare states. The debt crisis superficially confirms this view, but the reality is most of the debt was incurred by bailing out banks or preventing a global depression rather than by expanding the welfare state.

The neoliberal view sees social spending as a cost at the expense of prosperity. Its volume is limited by the revenue of tax and social contribution which is supposed to harm wealth creation if it is increased too much.

However, in real economic terms, costs mean a lower output and consumption of desired goods and services. As long as there are un- or underemployed people and opportunities to increase productivity, let alone export surpluses as in the case of Germany, there are no real costs. Output and consumption in other sectors will not be reduced, but will grow, too.[3] It is a problem of income distribution and structural change in the economy. Expanding industries providing social services such as education, health, and care or renewable energy will spur growth by creating jobs and increase productivity. The revenue needed to finance the supply will come either through markets or through public spending. The growing wage and profit income will lead to more demand for all kinds of goods and services and higher state revenues (tax and social security contributions).[4]

In a more equal society prosperity (in terms of access to private and public goods and services) could be based much more on markets and private enterprise as demand would be fuelled by broadly spread decent incomes. The less the poor can afford to buy these goods and services, the more they must be either provided as public goods and services or the incomes of the poor must be supplemented by cash transfers or vouchers. Protecting the population against risks (sickness, disability, old age etc.) will often involve

---

[3] See also Baumol, William J. (2012), *The Cost Disease: Why Computers Get Cheaper and Health Care Doesn't*, New Haven and London: Yale University Press.

[4] A model calculation done in the context of the FES project on "Social Growth" simulated the additional employment of almost one million people in the care economy leading to a rise of GDP by about 26 billion Euros. The expansion was based on multiplier effects and higher care insurance. See: http://library.fes.de/pdf-files/wiso/08886.pdf.

insurance. Again, public systems which prevent adverse selection and reduce overheads (costs of advertising and commissions) are likely to be more efficient than a plethora of competing private companies. More generally, the growth of the public sector reflects differences in productivity growth between sectors/activities and shifting societal preferences.

Conclusion

Social growth is based on the expansion of supply which satisfies the needs of the whole society rather than just a rich minority. It is also more sustainable as it does not have to rely on debt as much as the old growth model and it also uses fewer resources per unit of GDP. Eventually, in the case of Germany, such a new growth pattern would contribute to resolving the Euro crisis by correcting the German current account imbalances.

Editors

Gustav A. Horn is Director of the Macroeconomic Policy Institute (IMK) at the Hans–Böckler Foundation, a trade union related foundation. He is a permanent adviser to the German trade union movement. He is an external Professor at both the Universities of Flensburg and Duisburg-Essen. He is a member of various political committees and an advisor to the SPD, the European Parliament and the Green Party in the German Bundestag. He is also chairman of the Committee on Social Order of the Protestant Church in Germany. He holds the equivalent of a M.Sc. from the University of Bonn, an M.Sc. degree from the London School of Economics, and a Ph.D. from TU Berlin. Many of his recent policy papers are available on the IMK website at www.imk-boeckler.de.

Thomas I. Palley is Senior Economic Policy Adviser to the AFL-CIO. He is the author of numerous academic and popular articles and his most recent books are: *Financialization: The Economics of Finance Capital Domination* (Palgrave/Macmillan, 2013); *The Economic Crisis: Notes from the Underground* (Createspace, 2013); and *From Financial Crisis to Stagnation: The Destruction of Shared Prosperity and the Role of Economics* (Cambridge University Press, 2012). He holds a B.A. degree from Oxford University and a M.A. degree in International Relations and Ph.D. in Economics, both from Yale University. Many of his writings and op-eds on economic policy are available at www.thomaspalley.com

Made in the USA
Lexington, KY
09 January 2014